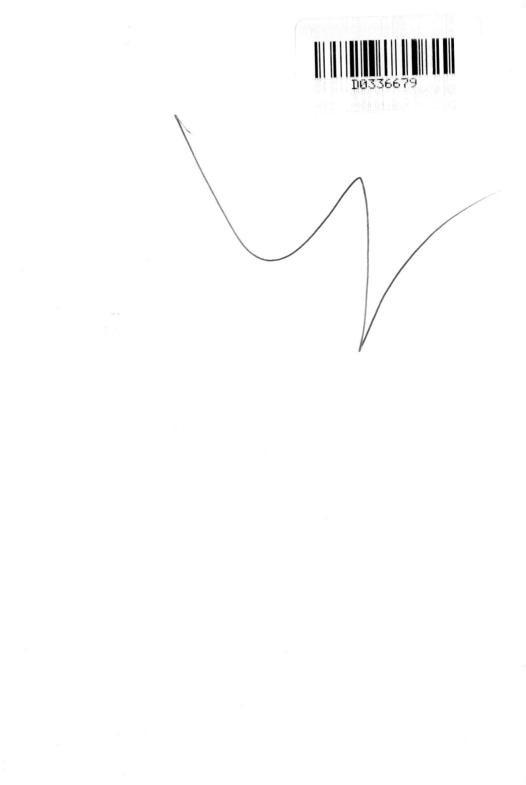

Mum Stuff

Love to Alison & Jake

Mum Stuff

Because Mum Knows Best

by Morag Cuddeford-Jones

Illustrations by Sue Hellard

SIMON &
SCHUSTER

London • New York • Sydney • Toronto

First published in Great Britain by Simon & Schuster UK Ltd, 2007
A CBS Company

1   3   5   7   9 10   8   6   4   2

Simon & Schuster UK Ltd
Africa House
64-78 Kingsway
London WC2B 6AH

www.simonsays.co.uk

Simon & Schuster Australia
Sydney

A CIP catalogue record for this book is available from the British Library

ISBN 10: 1 8473 7025 X
ISBN 13: 978 1 8473 7025 9

Illustrations by Sue Hellard
Practical illustrations by Liane Payne
Designed by Lovelock & Co.
Printed and bound in Great Britain by CPI Bath

Contents

Introduction

Mums know everything. Why else, any time they're asked a tricky question, would dads say, 'Ask your mother'?

The art of being a mum isn't really rocket science. Wipe a snotty nose here, patch up a grazed knee there, fill up empty tummies and keep everything ticking over nicely. But is that all there is? Surely, being a mum is a bit more, well, fun than that?

If women's lib showed us anything, it's that there's absolutely no reason to be chained to the kitchen sink or the oven and that there is more to life than a perfectly creased sleeve. With all the energy we've saved by sending the kids to school in fashionably rumpled shirts, we can get round to enjoying – rather than enduring – being a mum.

And that's where 'Mum Stuff' comes in. It is a collection of all the stuff we used to play as kids, the things we enjoyed doing and the things our parents enjoyed doing with us. Some of them have a modern twist, others are old favourites, and there are some typical 'mum skills' that have been lost to some of us.

This is less of a 'how-to' book, and more a 'Have you thought of ...?' When it's pouring with rain and the kids are getting on your nerves, flick through for some inspiration. I'm also a firm believer that for every minute you spend as 'quality time' (ooh, that phrase gives me hives) with your children, they need to spend an equal amount of quality time with themselves. That's why there are activities they can do on their own. And if that activity somehow results in the garden being tidied, shelves getting organised or homework being done, all the better.

Some of it's fun stuff, some of it's practical stuff, some of it's just downright silly stuff. But overall, it's just 'Mum Stuff'.

Guilty secrets

Before you get the idea that I wrote this book because I'm some kind of cross between Shirley Conran's Superwoman and Nigella Lawson's Domestic Goddess, let me set the record straight. Here is a list of dirty little secrets that prove I'm just as harried and distracted as the next woman. Possibly significantly more so.

- I have gone to the supermarket in my pyjamas.
- I have repaired my 'smart' work clothes with the following: pins, superglue, nail polish, garden twine, my husband's tie and sellotape.
- I use the dishwasher as a kitchen cupboard, rarely taking anything out to actually put it away.
- I told my mother-in-law that a stain on the carpet was made by a friend who concealed the evidence until it was too late to get it out. In reality it was caused by my son weeing on the floor and I just couldn't be bothered to clean it up.
- I have licked a spoon clean and put it straight back in the drawer.

Little virtues

But before you think of calling social services, I do have one or two redeeming features:

- I almost always cook dinner from scratch using fresh ingredients, (even if Mr Waitrose washed and chopped the veg for me).
- I take the opportunity while bathing my son to clean the bathroom. Because he gets a bath every day, the bathroom is cleaned every day so it takes seconds to do.
- I do a little bit of patchwork quilt on the train to and from the office. It uses up dead time constructively and it means I've got a priceless personal present for my grandmother's birthday.
- If I have the ingredients to hand, I'll make cupcakes in the morning for elevenses at work. I get lots of brownie points (excuse the pun!).
- I can make a working miniature carousel from an egg box, a pencil and a cheese-spread tub.
- I can quack like Donald Duck.

Enjoy.

Morag Cuddeford-Jones

Chapter One

Some paper stuff

t's amazing what you can do with a single bit of paper. You can make flying birds, fortune-tellers, boats, hats – and even books. Handier still is the fact that you're rarely without a piece. There's always a freebie newspaper or bit of junk mail knocking about that you can while away the hours with. Here are a few easy projects to make from paper.

Easy bishop's hat

Take a sheet of newspaper and fold it in half along the crease. Fold each top corner diagonally into the middle from the centre of the top fold, leaving a couple of inches untouched at the bottom open end. Fold the first (there are two from when you first folded the newspaper in half) leftover edge up and turn the paper over. Fold the narrow outside edges over a couple of inches, leaving a gap wide enough to get your head in, and fold the remaining leftover edge up. Put on head.

Paper flowers

Because of the floaty, flowery nature of these flowers, A4 office paper really won't cut it this time. But, never fear, you still don't need to rush out to the arts and crafts shop. Just use kitchen towel or loo roll instead.

Alternatively, the thin paper inside newspaper supplements will also fold well. Of course, if you follow my advice and become a master of the mum art of squirrelling (see page 231), your cupboard will be full to bursting with all the fancy coloured tissue posh shops wrap new clothes in.

To make a flower, layer several sheets of paper one on top of the other and cut a circle. It's easy to get a perfect circle, even if you don't have a ruler, compass or scissors. Simply fold whatever shape of paper you have in half, fold in half again. Cut an arc across the page between two corners on the diagonal. Unfold and Bob's your whatnot.

Keeping the circles together, fold them all in half then in half again. Pinch the bottom point and tease out layers of paper, gradually exposing the 'petals'. Keep going until you have a full flower head. For a stalk, use a straw, pipe cleaner, stick – anything that is thin enough, but still relatively rigid. Tie on with string or a couple of rounds of sellotape. Make lots and plant them in the flower border.

Snowflakes/Doilies

Another use for the circle pattern is to make snowflakes or copies of those paper doilies that gran insists on putting under her teapot. Fold a square of paper in half, in half again, then in half along the diagonal to make a triangle, then fold the triangle in half again lengthways. Cut off the 'tail' that's sticking out the end, and you'll have a long, thin isosceles triangle. At this point, DO NOT UNFOLD!

Instead, use scissors to 'nip' small shapes out of the edges. Triangles will give diamonds, arcs will give circles, and so on. Make deeper, bigger cuts at the shortest side of the triangle, possibly cutting the corners off to leave a small point. This will make it more flake-like. When you've chopped all you think you can, unfold and there's your snowflake.

Chinese lantern

Probably more appropriate at Chinese New Year, but we always had these dangling around the house at Christmas. Fold a piece of paper in half lengthways. A couple of inches in, start cutting slits along the fold about a centimetre apart, stopping a couple of inches from the other end, and about an inch from the long edge. Open out and then bring the short ends together and fix with glue or sellotape. Cut a small strip of paper for a handle and fix to the sides at one end. Decorate and hang up. If you can, hang a low-wattage, bulb, such as a fairy light, inside the lantern but do NOT use candles or high-wattage bulbs unless you quite literally fancy going up like a Christmas tree.

Paper mats

If you can get your hands on some A3 paper, it's just the right shape for a table mat. Obviously, a plain bit of office paper is a boring table mat so we need to go about decorating it.

Fold the paper lengthways and cut it in much the same way as you did your Chinese lantern. As the straightness of your cutting will determine the neatness of your finished product, you might want to be a bit more precise this time, and measure the slits out with a ruler.

Next, get your hands on some different coloured strips of paper the same length as the height of the large bit of paper and a centimetre or so wide. Traditionally, the strips are split into two colours but you can be as creative as you like. Use old bits of wallpaper, cut up magazines etc. Weave the strips in and out of the slats on the big piece of paper. Make sure there are no gaps between the strips by pushing them gently together. To make it extra secure, glue the ends of the strips down onto the piece of A3 when you've finished weaving, and trim them to make them neat.

Paper finger puppets

Ideally, to make these puppets, you'll need slightly stiffer material than just ordinary paper, but you can use anything from cereal packets to magazine covers. The latter are particularly handy if you need to break up a really boring train or plane journey. Simply cut (or tear) the outline of your puppet. It should be at least the size of your palm with a good wide base. This is because you need to have enough space at the bottom to poke two holes for two of your fingers to fit through.

If you don't have scissors handy, it can be tricky to make the holes, but here's a tip: fold the puppet gently in half where the middle of your finger is going to go, then slowly and gently tear a semicircle. When you open it up there should be a circle for you to stick your fingers through.

These puppets lend themselves particularly well to cancan routines so puppets should be adorned accordingly. Loud renditions of cancan music are not advised in the 'Quiet' train carriage and will see you slung out at Crewe. Not a lot happens in Crewe.

Sick-bag puppets

These days it's getting harder and harder to take anything into the cabin of an aeroplane so it's lucky that the airlines helpfully supply neat little sick bags to make puppets from.

Turn the bag upside down. They usually have square, folded bases. Fold the two front corners of the base under themselves to create a jawline for the face. From the back of the bag, just below the base (it would normally be above, but you should have the whole thing upside down by now), tear out two triangles, or semi-circles but make sure you leave the side that attaches them to the base untorn. Fold them so they stick up. Do the same with the sides of the bag to create arms and legs. From an unobtrusive bit at the back of the bag, tear off another triangle shape completely, and fold it in half. Poke a little hole through the base where the mouth should be and thread the triangle through, point first from inside the bag. Flatten out the triangle a bit and there's your tongue. All you need to do to finish off your puppet is beg the stewardess for a pen and draw on the rest of the features.

Paper-chain people

Paper chains are great fun, both for the challenge of getting as many in a row as possible, and also for seeing who has the strongest fingers to get the scissors to cut through wads and wads of folded paper.

Simply take whatever paper you have to hand (the bigger it is, the longer the chain – newspaper is good) and fold it like a fan, with each fold being equal size and the exact width of the drawing you want to cut out.

Draw the design onto the front of the folded paper, making sure the left and right sides of the drawing are both touching the far edges of the folds. Cut round the top and the bottom of the drawing, leaving as much of the left and right sides of the drawing uncut as possible. Unfold the fan and marvel at your magnificent multiplication.

Christmas stars

These are a little bit fiddly at first, and you can get caught out if your strip of paper isn't long enough but, practice makes perfect!

Start with a strip of paper about 1cm wide by 30cm long. Tie a loose knot in one end, taking care not to crease the paper, leaving a tail of about 5cm at the end. When you've got the knot as tight as you can without crushing the paper, press it flat gently. You should see a pentagon, the foundation of the star shape.

Fold the long tail round and round the pentagon (it will automatically cover all the sides), tucking the remaining bits inside a convenient gap. Start pushing in the sides of the pentagon, going round and round with your finger pushing a little more in at a time. The centre should start to rise out and the shape of the star become evident. When you think you're as popped and pushed as you can go, pinch the star points to make them sharper. Decorate as you see fit and dangle from the tree.

Papier-mâché

Papier-mâché is a handy, gloopy substance made with newspaper and some household cooking ingredients that you can use to mould round any object. When it dries it becomes a 'shell' of the object that you can then turn into anything you fancy. Obviously, if you make a shell of a cup then you've made another cup, but using something as anonymous as a balloon means you've got a couple of semi-circles to use for anything. The only limit is your imagination.

Papier-mâché paste

Always use 1 part flour to 3 parts water.

Whisk a cup of flour with a cup of water and mix well. Add another two cups of flour and beat out the lumps. Bring to the boil in a pan. Keep stirring. Don't cook it too hard or long or it will be too thick. Cool and store in a covered container in the fridge. It lasts almost a week.

Many kids of my generation used wallpaper paste for papier-mâché. This as it turns out, was a bad idea as apparently it's quite toxic.

To use: Tear newspaper into smallish strips and squares. You can use largeish bits to cover big areas but don't make them too big or it isn't as strong. Brush paste onto the object you're moulding; for example, a balloon can make a piggy bank or be cut in half when set to make two bowls. Layer on the bits of newspaper. Wait until one layer is dry, then repeat. Three to four layers is usually enough for a small object; if it's big or going to get a lot of handling (like a plate or piggy bank) you could need up to eight.

Because of the drying time in between layers and coats, it can take a few days to finish the whole project. It'll teach 'em patience.

Top tip: Don't be tempted to dry it next to a radiator or in an oven. It'll either go a funny shape or burst into flames.

To get rid of the balloon, simply pop with a pin through the hardened paper. If you want the mould to remain whole, you can just leave the balloon inside, or make a small nick somewhere and try 'hooking' it out with a skewer or chopstick. If you are planning to cut the mould in half, then you can easily remove the balloon afterwards.

Unless you like the newsprint look, you'll want to paint the object. To make sure paint doesn't soak in, prime it with 2 parts PVA glue to 1 part water for bright colours. White emulsion works better if you're going to paint it in white or pastel colours. Once that's dried, you can start painting. Acrylic is best and doesn't smudge if you want to varnish it. Of course, you don't need to varnish it but it helps the item last longer and gives kids one more thing to get on with before they bother you for something else to do.

To varnish, mix PVA glue with about as quarter as much water as in the primer. It goes on cloudy but dries clear. Cover it a few times, allowing drying time between coats.

Papier-mâché piñata

Blow up a big balloon – the bigger the better. Apply your paper strips and paste all over until you have about four layers, remembering to let each layer dry before adding the next. Decorate however you fancy, but the more extravagant the better with bright colours and ribbons.

Pop the balloon with a pin and cut a small unobtrusive opening somewhere, then fill with goodies such as sweets. Attach some string firmly to the piñata and hang it from a tree.

Blindfold one child at a time, hand them a stick and let them have one or two swings at the piñata. The one who manages to burst the piñata, causing a shower of sweets and goodies from on high, is the winner.

Games with a piece of paper ...and a pen

Consequences

The aim is to come up with a story together, by each secretly writing a sentence or drawing a picture. If there are a group of you – at least four is ideal – you can play this game with hilarious consequences. Tear an A4 sheet of paper into four strips, or to match the number of people playing.

Each player takes a sheet.

For the writing version, the first person writes the opening line to a story at the top of the paper. Important: do this in total secrecy. No one must guess what you're writing. When you've finished, fold the paper in half so that your part is obscured from the next person's view, but so that the next thing they add will be just below yours. Repeat the steps until you've run out of players or space on the paper.

For the drawing version, draw a head at the top of the paper, fold this over to conceal what you've drawn from the next person. They then draw a torso and pass on, and so on until the feet have been drawn.

Then take turns to unfold the sheets of paper and read out or demonstrate the results.

Who am I?

Played with Post-it notes in the party games chapter (see page 139) or Rizla papers in the grown-ups version, you can also play this with small bits of paper torn from anywhere to brighten up a train journey. Write the name of a famous person on a piece of paper and swap with someone else. Show the piece of paper that you've received to everyone but yourself, then ask questions, one at a time, to find out who you are. The first person to guess who they are is the winner.

Secret writing

If there's one thing kids are good at, it's passing notes in class. If there's another thing they're good at, it's getting caught. These tricks won't necessarily stop them getting caught but it might save them the embarrassment of the whole class finding out that they fancy Bob from 6B.

Method number one is to get hold of a sharpened carrot and a bowl of squeezed lemon juice. Using the carrot as a pen, dip it in the lemon juice and write the message as normal. But where is the writing?! Hold the piece of paper up to a gentle heat source, such as a warm radiator or, if very careful, a hob on low heat. The lemon juice should turn brown in the heat and the message will be revealed.

Method number two involves candles and crayons and less opportunity to burn the house down. Using a white candle, write your message on a piece of paper. But, *zut alors!* Still there is no writing! Take a dark crayon, colouring pencil or pen and lightly colour in wide strokes across the paper. Because the colour won't stick to the candlewax, the message will soon be revealed.

A movie in your pocket

This is a good project for when the kids are bored on a plane or train. The paper you need doesn't even have to be blank; it can be a novel, a diary, a pamphlet or a magazine. All you need is a sliver of white space at the edge of the page, and a decent number of pages to make it 'flickable' (you'll soon see why).

Choose a simple cartoon picture that represents something that changes shape when it moves. For example, an animal, a bird or a person. Objects such as cars aren't great because they don't change shape when they move. However, the scenery around them does so you can change that instead. It just means a bit more drawing for them (and more peace and quiet for you).

Draw the figure in one pose on the last sheet of paper. Then draw the same figure on the next but last sheet, only with a slight difference.

For example, if it's a stick man with both arms down, then this time draw him with one arm up. Then on the next page, keep the arm up and move the leg up. Keep going until you run out of pages, or ideas. When you've finished all the pictures, close the magazine, hold the pages tightly closed and use your thumb to flick the pages from back to front. Your figure will start to jig around and should amaze and astound the kids enough to try out lots of versions of their own.

The trickier stuff: origami

The Japanese art of origami sounds very classy but horribly complicated. It's not. You just have to make sure you follow instructions and understand them before you start. This is a mum's job. Dads are pathologically unable to follow instructions as many of us know to our cost. This is why dads' relationship with origami is limited to trying to fold a sheet of paper in half seven times before giving up and blaming the 'wrong sort' of paper. Mums know that by simply reading instructions you can keep kids fascinated for hours and demonstrate that you are, in fact, some kind of genius into the bargain.

Before you start, you almost always need to use a perfectly square piece of paper. Unfortunately, most spare paper knocking around the house these

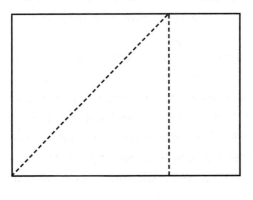

days tends to be A4 size. All is not lost. Instead of lots of complex measuring, marking and cutting, just use this simple technique.

Lie the paper in a landscape format (long bit at the bottom). Pick up the top left corner and fold it diagonally to touch the bottom of the long side. The two edges should now match each other. There should be a rectangular remnant sticking out the end. Fold the rectangular edge over so the effect is a triangle. Unfold the triangle so that you now have a square with a rectangular flap. If you're not confident about your tearing skills, use something with a straight edge such as a ruler to rip the flap off. Otherwise, just make sure the fold is sharp (run your nail up and down it) and tear slowly. Voila!, a square piece of paper.

The fortune-teller

I learnt this with my girlfriends in primary school and it was a fad for ages. We made them over and over again.

1   Valley fold (that is, fold both sides up towards you so that the fold is at the bottom) the opposite corners together, in turn, to mark the diagonal fold lines, and open them up.
2   Fold all corners into the middle. Turn the paper over.
3   Fold all corners into the middle again.
4   Fold the paper in half along the valley fold lines, and in half again along the valley folds until you have a small square.
5   Open up these two folds and turn over to see the four thumb and forefinger flaps.
6   Insert thumb and forefinger into these flaps and pinch them and bring hands together.
7   Opening thumbs and forefingers shows one view of the inside, moving your hands a small distance apart reveals another. To prove this, open up the fortune-teller again and write numbers one to eight on the triangles on the inside flaps. One view will show three, four, seven and eight; the other shows one, two, five and six.

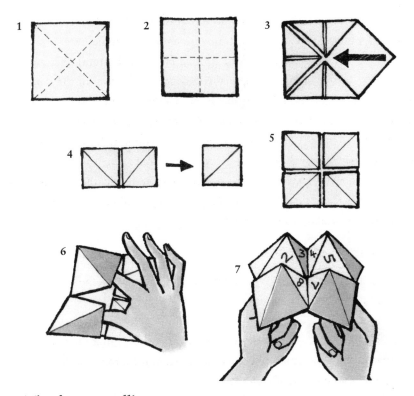

The fortune-telling game

We would decorate our fortune-tellers with colours, numbers, phrases and predictions. You then pick a 'customer' who has to pick a colour first – one of the four on your thumb flaps. You alternate the opening and closing mechanism (move your fingers apart, then your hands, then fingers, then hands etc.) as you spell the colour. The last letter reveals which set of numbers the customer can pick from. They choose a number and the above step is repeated, with counting instead of spelling. This reveals the number set again. The customer picks another number and this time you open up the fortune teller and lift the flap with the number on it. This reveals their fortune: "Gary from 4B will ask you out", or some such nonsense.

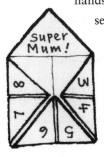

Chapter Two

Some crafty stuff

With a bit of luck and some hunting around, you can always find stuff knocking around the house for crafts. Whether it's a school project the kids have left to the last minute or simply that they've been driving you nuts by saying, 'I'm bored …' every five minutes, you can always find something for them to make or do.

Admittedly, some projects require a bit of adult input. If you can't rope a spare dad or older sibling into taking over then you may even have to get stuck in yourself (see Chapter Three for some really hands-off activities). Unfortunately, you might find them quite absorbing and the children could end up complaining that mum won't let them have a go …

Pasta jewellery

This simple activity can keep younger children occupied for hours. And, yes, it extends to boys as well. You may want to keep their efforts for proud display when they bring their first girlfriend round.

All you need is string and some tube-shaped pasta. There are lots of varieties that come in tubes; spirals add a bit of variety, but are admittedly a bit of a beggar to thread, especially for those with little fingers. You could invest in the coloured varieties of dried pasta but they aren't the brightest colours, so let the kids use poster paints, glitter, glue and stickers instead.

Making earrings for little ones is a bit tricky, but you could try dangling a spiral off a small loop, then hooking it over their ears to help them 'complete the look'. Sweetie, dahling.

To dye for

Instead of flying into a flat panic when the kids insist on making like Jackson Pollock with blackcurrant juice, why not embrace their creative tendencies. Instead of scrubbing out tea stains, add to them. Embrace your inner slobberer. A warning: dye won't just colour your bit of cloth, it colours anything it touches. This includes hands, your clothes, your carpet and anything else unlucky enough to get in the way, so remember to wear rubber gloves and don't wear Sunday best to go tie-dyeing in. If you use plastic or melamine tubs to mix the dye, it will more than likely colour them too. Good containers are glass or porcelain, which are glazed and won't take the colour. Don't wash dyed items with other clothes as the colour will run. Also, check that the ingredients you're using, especially garden ones, aren't poisonous.

Kitchen-cupboard colourings

Making and using homemade dyes is great fun for kids and adults alike. There's lots of steaming pots, using up of leftovers and general mucking about without too much clearing up afterwards.

Red cabbage

Chop a couple of red cabbages into quarters and boil for an hour. Strain off the veg and soak the cloth in the liquid overnight. Even if the water is a livid purple, the effect is still not startlingly bright. However, it does shine through if you can find 'unmordanted' cloth, that is, one that hasn't had a colour fix already. Raw cottons and anything from a stall staffed by dreadlocked students should do the trick.

My Scottish grandmother complains that this is a waste of perfectly good vegetables. She'd claim that cooking a cabbage for an hour made it inedible. It would be way too undercooked. She's the same about sprouts.

Onions – red and white (which are actually yellow)

Collect as many onion skins as you can over the course of the week. Keep them in an open container in a dry place to stop them going mouldy. Cover with water and simmer for an hour until the skins have lost all their colour. Add wet cloth to the mix and simmer for another hour. You can get even darker colours if you leave it to cool down in the pan overnight.

Coffee

The explosion in mocha-choca-latte-double-decaff-espresso-latte shops means that there's an excess of used coffee grounds going begging. Some chains package it up and leave it to be collected for free; otherwise just ask for it. In the first place, it makes a really good compost, but, used coffee also makes a good tan or beige dye. You can also use it on muslin to 'age' it. Make a strong pot of coffee, then tip into a bowl and add the cloth (leave the grounds in the water as they wash off easily) until you have the colour you want.

Bilberries and blueberries

During the First World War, you couldn't find bilberries or blueberries to eat (see page 89 for jam) for love nor money because they were all being used for dark-blue or purple dye. The UK used to get this colour from aniline dye imported from Germany and obviously that wasn't an option any more!

Another way of getting dark-blue is to use the Indigo plant. All you have to do is go to Africa where it's grown, gather several litres of human pee and ferment it in a barrel at the bottom of your garden for six weeks then boil the indigo plant and the item you want to colour for a few hours so that it 'takes'. The first few wearings of your newly dyed item might want to be accessorised with hefty applications of perfume.

Experiment with other household and garden items such as cranberries, blackberries, turmeric, beetroot and lettuce. Because you're not dyeing professionally, the colour is unlikely to last too long, especially if you wash it in modern detergent afterwards. Remember, these guys make it their business to get stuff out that you've spent the best part of two days putting in!

Tie-dye (and shirt-dye and skirt-dye and even vest-dye)

One of the best things to do with all this dye you've made is a spot of tie-dyeing. Not limited to hippies in the 1970s, tie-dye clothes still have their place. Granted, that place is mostly under six layers of mud at Glastonbury, but it shows willing.

Tie-dyeing is a simple technique and does pretty much what it says on the tin. You tie up a bit of cloth and then you dye it. The most commonly used technique is to get a number of smallish stones and tie some cloth around them using string. If you tie the string nice and tightly, the less likely dye will get into the piece of cloth underneath it. The more times you wind the string round, the more cloth you'll cover, therefore the bigger the area that won't be dyed. And this is the point of the technique. You're working in negative, trying to dye everything BUT the pattern you're making.

The tying-round-a-stone technique will give you a big, fuzzy white (if the original cloth was white) circle on a dyed background. Tying lots of stones of different sizes will give you lots of white circles of different sizes.

You can also make a kind of zig-zag pattern by folding the cloth up in a concertina shape, ironing the creases nice and sharp and clamping them at intervals with strong bulldog clips. Folding the cloth in four and then winding thread down it in a spiral will make a kind of thin petal effect.

You can even sew a few lines of tacking (see page 226) across the cloth and then, instead of finishing with a double stitch, just leave a length of thread hanging out off the end. When you have the number of rows you want, pull all the threads so that the cloth crumples and gathers up into tight folds. Pull nice and tight to stop dye getting into all the creases and when you've finished, there will be a nice fine pattern going all the way across.

You don't have to stick to one pattern. You can have circles with fine lines running round them, and a petal pattern at the edges. Once you've finished all the tying, it can look like you've just got a lumpy chunk of cloth, but it will be fine, I promise.

Give it two or three rinses to make sure all of the extra dye is out. Hang out to dry. It may look odd trying to dry it with all its lumps still in, but if you take all the string out while it's still wet, the dye might run into your carefully creased-up white bits.

Dyeing to see the result

If you're not going down the au naturel route of using homemade dyes, then the best shop-bought version is Dylon cold-water dye. The packet instructions are easy to follow – basically, you mix the dye in a bowl with hot water and add a tablespoon of salt. Then, pour it into a bigger tub and add cold water, stirring well. Wet the cloth before you add it to the dye and then leave for about an hour, stirring it every now and again to make sure it's evenly covered.

Batik

This works on a similar principle to tie-dye (see above), in that the aim is to create a pattern by keeping the dye off certain bits of the cloth. But it's in reverse in that the dye will be the pattern, surrounded by white bits. Instead of using string and pebbles, you use wax. It's a bit fiddlier than tie-dye but you can control the patterns you want to make, and paint pictures on the cloth.

It also involves a bit more equipment. First, you'll need a frame to hold your cloth steady so you can draw on it. You could make a frame by knocking together four bits of wood into a square, but it's easier to use an old picture frame, the bigger the better. Take out all the inside gubbins so you're just left with the frame (clip frames are no good for obvious reasons). Then, you'll need some drawing pins or similar. Dampen the cloth slightly and pin it flat over the frame. When the cloth dries it will shrink a little making it nice and taut and easy to draw on.

While it's drying, melt down a couple of white household candles. Put the candles in a heatproof container such as an old tin can, and then put it in a pan with a few centimetres of water (it should come almost halfway up the side of the can). This means the wax will melt gently without spitting or burning.

Once it's melted and the cloth is dry, paint the melted wax evenly over both sides of the cloth, making sure all of the cloth is covered. When the wax hardens (pretty much instantaneously), start scraping your pattern out. You need to remember to scrape the pattern out on both sides of the cloth so that the dye can work its way through.

Next, dye the cloth, using the same method as with tie-dye. When it's all dry, gently scrape away as much of the remaining wax as possible. Using brown paper (any thinnish, absorbent paper would do, but if you use newspaper the design might get covered in yesterday's news) and a warm iron, cover the cloth with the paper and gently iron back and forth so that the wax melts and comes off the cloth. You'll probably need to do this a few times, changing the paper so that all the wax gets absorbed.

Wash in warm soapy water a few times to get out the last of the dye and wax, dry and iron a final time. Step back and admire handiwork.

You can do batik to almost anything, but it works particularly well for wall hangings and headscarves. Perhaps granny would like a batik shawl for Christmas next year. It'll beat the lavender bath salts hands down (see page 42 for these!)

Eggstraspecial

You can use all of the dyeing techniques above to decorate eggs, which make great Easter decorations, naturally. Or you may just fancy decorating an egg.

Because of the nature of an egg, and its tendency to smell ... eggy after a while, the best way to decorate an egg if you want to keep it for any length of time is with its insides out. Unfortunately, the way to get them out is usually fairly fatal for the eggshell that you want to decorate. However, it is possible.

Prick the pointy end of the egg with a pin to make a small hole. Then use the pin to make a hole at the other end, gently chipping the edges to make the hole bigger. Hold the egg over a bowl with the large hole facing down, and poke the pin through the hole once more to make sure you've broken the membrane that holds all the insides together. Now take a big breath and blow through the small hole. The contents should slither out. After all of the contents are in the bowl, rinse the shell in water and let it dry before you decorate it.

My gran used to make a very simple egg dye by putting the egg in boiling water along with a coloured paper napkin for about 15 minutes, but you can also use the homemade dyes on the previous pages.

Cloth, string and wool

Making stuff from cloth, string and wool is rewarding because on the whole it lasts longer than things made from paper and card. Sometimes they even have a practical use. Cloth can be used to make trousers, for example, which can hide your knobbly knees from public view. Buttons can be used to hold said trousers up, or even be used as a pair of eyes on Slithersome, the sassy, secretive sock puppet.

Snake puppets

Using an old sock, put your hand inside and 'suck' the end into your palm to make a mouth. Mark on the top of your hand where you want the eyes and forked tongue to go. It doesn't have to be a snake – socks make good dinosaur heads, too. Add whatever features you want such as buttons for eyes, and cloth for the tongue. Sew the face onto the sock et voila!

Sock people

If you're bored of your sock puppet, you can turn it into a little person instead. Cut vertically halfway through the foot of the sock from bridge to arch. Sew running stitch all the way round the open end, about a centimetre from the top, leaving the ends loose. Fill the sock with a stuffing of your choice. It could be cotton wool, or it could be some of our trusty chopped-up tights. Pull the ends of your running stitch tight to close the opening, tie them together in a tight knot and cut the ends down so you can't see the join.

Sew two small buttons on about halfway down the sock for the eyes. Cut about 10–15 lengths of wool for the 'hair' (enough to cover the head from one side to the other). Tack across the top of the head using small stitches to gather in mid-point of each length of wool. For speed, sew over three or four lengths of wool in one go. Cut two foot shapes from some light cardboard, colour in and glue to the bottom of your sock person.

Bobbles

Cut two pieces of sturdy cardboard (from a delivery box for example), into two circles as wide as you want your bobble to be. Cut out a circle in the middle, so you have doughnut-shaped pieces of card. The hole needs to be at least as large as three thumbs worth otherwise it will be hard to get the wool through. Wrap the wool round and round the rings until all the cardboard is covered up and the hole in the middle is nearly full. It doesn't have to be the same coloured wool. Use more than one colour for multi-coloured bobbles.

Use a pair of scissors to push the blade under the wool on the outer circle, getting between the two pieces of card. Cut along the top of the circle. Slip a length of wool between the two bits of card and tie the circle in the middle. Wind the wool around a couple of times to make sure it doesn't break, and leave a 'tail' so you can attach your bobble to something. When you've got the string tied nice and tight, pull the bits of cardboard off and fluff up the bobble. Stick it on anything you feel needs bobbled, or give it to the cat to chase.

Tassels

Using a small box or piece of card, wind the wool around several times, depending on how thick you want your tassel to be. The thickness on one side will be half the overall thickness of your tassel. Cut through the wool at one end, fold it in half so that all the ends meet. Wind another length of wool round and round about 2cm down from the folded part to create a loop. Tie the ends to secure it and trim.

Weaving

Using the same strong cardboard, cut a rectangle about the size of your hand, but you can make it as big as you like really. Chop the ends into a zig-zag. This is your loom. Wrap some wool (you can also use string, ribbon, wire – anything that bends) round the card, in between the teeth of the zig-zag and tie together.

Either make a needle out of cardboard, or use one of those nice, big, blunt tapestry needles that you use to sew up knitting. Thread your needle with wool and work in and out of the wool on the loom. After each row, push it down to fit neatly alongside the last one. Cut along the middle of the wool at the back of the loom to free up your square of cloth, or occasional rug for the doll's house, however you like to look at it.

To knit or not...

Not everyone who knits has blue-tinged hair and trouble operating the video recorder. Don't tell anyone, but being able to knit is becoming a bit – cool. The old-fashioned knitting circle has been given a bit of an update and now people are getting together for 'Stitch and Bitch' sessions, complete with glasses of wine and hot gossip.

Knowing how to knit is one of those 'mum skills' that it's great to have and pass on. The good thing about teaching kids to knit (yes, girls and boys) is that they can get some pretty instant gratification – once they've got over the initial frustration of tying themselves, the furniture and the cat into one big, woolly knot.

Casting on

This is a very basic form of casting on and doesn't give the most even hem, but it's good for complete beginners.

Make a looped knot at the end of a piece of wool. Slide it onto a needle, which you need to hold in your left hand, near the pointed end. Holding another needle in your right hand, slide it through the right-hand side of the loop until the needles form a cross. Bring the wool round between the two needles (lifting it from the back, over the top at the point where the needles cross and back down again).

1. bring wool between needles   2. hook wool through   3. transfer loop to left needle

Holding this length of wool quite tight alongside the needle in your right hand, push the right needle back and down a little way so that it hooks the wool that you just brought over between the cross. Move the tip of the right needle under the left, catching the wool on its way, so that you've made a second hoop. Transfer that second loop back onto the left needle so now you have two stitches sitting there. Push the right needle through the new loop and repeat the process, making a third, fourth, fifth stitch etc. To do some practice knitting, you only need to make about 10 stitches.

Knit

The casting-on stitch is basically the same as the knit stitch. The only difference with the knit stitch is that once you've got the second loop on the right needle, you pull away gently with the right hand until the loop nearest to the point on the left needle (i.e. the one you put your right needle through to make the second loop) falls off in between your two needles. You don't want to pull any more than that or you'll have a dropped stitch, and they're a pain to pick up again.

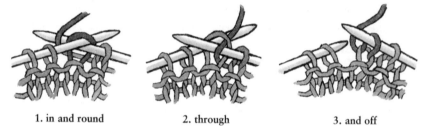

1. in and round   2. through   3. and off

If you knit the whole garment in this stitch, it will come out in a pattern called 'garter stitch'. This is the wavy pattern that you often see on the inside of shop-bought jumpers.

If you want to have the same look as a shop-bought jumper, you need to make the waves on the inside, but long lines of 'v's on the outside. This is called 'stocking stitch' and it's the way most jumpers, gloves, socks etc. are created. To do this, you need to knit one row in garter then every other row in 'purl'.

Purl

Purl is almost the exact opposite of knit. You need to make sure that your length of wool is always hanging down at the front of your needles instead of behind. You don't need to do anything special, just hold it there when you begin a row and the stitches will do the rest.

Now, instead of poking your right needle away from you through the left-hand row of stitches, you need to put it through the loop towards you.

Therefore, instead of putting the needle through the loop on its left side, you put it through on its right.

Once the right needle is poking out of the loop towards you, hook the length of wool round the right needle anticlockwise and pull tight. Pull the right needle back in the direction it came, ensuring that you

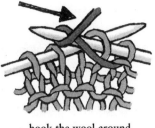

hook the wool around
the needle

slip the new loop of wool underneath the old one. Again, pull the needles gently apart until the old loop drops off the end of the left-hand needle.

For basic patterns, knit and purl are the only two stitches you really need to know.

Increasing

Unless you're making something box-shaped, you'll probably have to increase and decrease stitches at some point. Unlike cloth, which you can merrily cut to shape, doing the same to a bit of knitting will return it very swiftly to its ball-of-wool status, albeit unwound and in several small bits. So, you have to shape your material as you go.

To increase, you simply put the needle through as if to knit one stitch, lift the wool over and hook it round and under as normal. But instead of completing the move by pulling the stitch off the left-hand needle, you bring the right-hand needle up and over the point of the left-hand one and slide it through the back of the stitch you've just almost knitted. Still with me? Then 'knit' that bit as well. It might be a bit of a squeeze; try to relax the wool a bit to give yourself space, but by the time you pull the stitch off the left-hand needle, you now have two stitches for the price of one.

Decreasing

Often, patterns instruct you to decrease at both ends of the piece you're knitting. The bad news is this means two different techniques. The good news is they're dead simple.

You can either knit two together, which does exactly what it says on the tin. Stick the right-hand needle through not one but two stitches and knit as normal. You do exactly the same if it's a purl stitch. Alternatively, you cast one off using the technique below.

Casting off

Knit (or purl if that's where you are in the pattern) one stitch, then the next. Take the first stitch, lift it over the one you've just made, pull it off the end of the needle. If you want to cast off in one straight line, just keep going like this all the way along – knit, lift, drop – (remembering that you must not have more than two stitches on the right-hand needle at one time) until you only have one stitch left. Holding onto the knitted material, pull the needle with the stitch left on it up in the air making an enormous loop. Cut the wool close to the remainder of the ball and then pull the needle still further. The cut end will pop through, making the last stitch into an

lift the first stitch over
the second

instant tidy knot that'll stop it all unravelling. You want a nice long tail end because you can then use it to sew the seams up (if you have any), leaving a minimum of scraggly ends dangling off the inside.

Adding a new colour/new ball

For the sake of simplicity, I'll stick to adding colours in rows. It really is very, very easy. Just pick up your new ball of wool and get a good long dangly end. Holding it with the dangly end down, start knitting along the row as if nothing had changed. The only difference is that you're using a new ball of wool. This is exactly how you add a new ball of wool when you've run out of the old stuff. Even if it's exactly the same colour. You just hold onto the new thread and use that instead.

Knit a blanket

With your average pre-teen having the attention span of a gnat, expecting them to hunker down and knit a whole blanket from scratch is a bit like handing an infinite number of monkeys some paper and expecting Hamlet. Theoretically possible, in practice – *pfft!*

Doing a patchwork in bits is more manageable and gives you a much easier way of changing colour as you go along. It's also cheaper, as you can just grab single balls of wool from the discount basket.

Cast on 20 stitches. Knit the first row, purl the second. Keep going until you have what looks like a square, then cast off. Repeat with different colours until you have enough to make the size of blanket you want.

You need to sew all the bits together using the leftover wool. You don't necessarily need a special needle, but most knitters use a tapestry needle, which is big and blunt and has a huge eye (hole). Department stores sell them and they cost pence. Heard the phrase 'getting a camel through the eye of a needle'? Well it's a similar experience trying to get chunky Aran through an ordinary sewing needle.

Sew along all the sides of your wool squares, double stitching every time you come to a corner, or the end of your thread. This helps stop it unravelling. Once finished, stand back, admire your handiwork and rub moisturiser into your calloused index finger.

Knit a scarf

Scarves are exceedingly easy to make. You don't have to worry about them being too long (we have Tom Baker's *Doctor Who* to thank for that) and there's no shaping.

Cast on 50 stitches (it doesn't matter if it's 48 or 52, just try to end with the same number as you started with). Knit one row, purl the next and so on for what seems like an eternity. Holding the needle with a whole row on it, you can wrap the scarf round your neck to see how you're doing.

An alternative is to do the scarf in rib pattern. It's very easy. Rib is the pattern on the waistband and cuffs of most jumpers, and it's a common way of knitting scarves. It means that the scarf has the same pattern on both sides because, unlike a jumper, it's very probable that you will see both sides of the scarf when it's being worn, so you want both sides to look nice.

Rib is simply knit one, purl one, knit one, purl one, but every stitch instead of every row. You won't want it that fine, so an ideal pattern is to knit two, purl two and repeat all the way along. You want to do the exact opposite on the following row, so if you end on two knit stitches, you need to start by doing two purl stitches. So it goes:

Row 1: K2,P2,K2,P2 ... end on K2
Row 2: P2,K2,P2,K2 ... end on P2
Row 3: K2,P2,K2,P2 ... end on K2

It may seem as though you're going to have to really concentrate all the way through knitting the scarf, rather than just mindlessly clacking along with garter or stocking stitch, but you soon get into a rhythm.

When you've finished, cast off. To add the final *je ne sais quoi*, you could sew some of the tassels we made earlier onto each end of the scarf.

Making dough

Soft playdough

The bought stuff is really expensive, gets stuck in all sorts of crevices and goes hard if you leave the lid off. The homemade stuff does exactly the same thing, except it's cheap as chips and you can make more and more and more. In a saucepan, mix 100g plain flour, 150g salt, 2 tbsp cream of tartar, 2 tbsp vegetable oil and 8 fl oz water with food colouring of choice. Stir it over a medium heat until it all comes together in one dough ball. When it's cool, knead it till it's soft then store it somewhere airtight. Don't let children feed the dough to animals as it may be harmful.

Hard playdough

This is more of a clay-type mix that can be baked in the oven to preserve the little darlings' creations for eternity. Mix 400g plain flour and 2 tbsp salt with enough water to make a firm dough – you don't want it sticky. Let the kids make what they like out of it. Put the models on a baking sheet and into the oven at about 150°C (any higher and they'll crack and disintegrate, any lower and it will take for ever) until they're dry. Leave to cool then paint. You could colour the dough at the mixing stage using food colouring but this means you won't be able to paint the models afterwards.

Crafty Christmas

There's nothing mums and grandmas appreciate more than crafty gifts made with love. Actually, that's a lie. What we really like is a voucher for a fabulous spa with an invitation to drink as much bubbly as we like. Failing that, however, we'll put up with a homemade offering once in a while.

Bath salts

If we're not going to get the full spa treatment, at least we can treat ourselves to a soak in the bath. It's pretty easy to make some nice smelling bath salts, and also surprising how nice you can make the whole thing look. You won't be able to find all the ingredients you need around the house, but the local chemist should have them for pennies.

Mix 2 cups of Epsom salts with 1 cup of coarse sea salt. Stir in 2–3 drops of food colouring. Then add 6 drops of essential oil and stir again. When it's all combined, tip it into a big jar, or even a small vase. Cover with some nice fabric and tie with a ribbon.

For maximum impact, make a few batches using different food colourings, then layer them one on top of the other. Stick to the same essential oil, though, or the combination of smells could be quite overpowering.

Making candles

A word of warning: the hot bit of this activity will need a lot of adult input. But kids join in by collecting all the remnants, and they can set up the wick. All mum has to do is the melty, pouring bit. With supervision, kids can remove the mould and tie pretty ribbons around the candles.

Smelly candles are the lifestyle accessory du jour. And don't marketing people know it. The average posh candle costs nearly as much as a three-course meal for two and lasts about a week. And the wick almost always burns out before the wax does, leaving you staring at a bread basket's worth of candle that you can't do anything with.

Unless ... you can always reform the candle into a smaller shape so you can get some more burning time out of it. Polystyrene cups or those plastic ones you get with watercoolers are a good shape to reconstitute your candle. Unfortunately, you can't use any old string as a wick, but it's quite easy to get hold of candlewick from hobby shops, department stores and even online.

You need to weight the candlewick at the bottom of the cup. You could try sticking it to the bottom with some glue, sellotape or a bit of Blu-tack. String it so that it stays vaguely in the middle of the candle. If you don't, it'll slope to the side and won't burn the candle evenly.

To do this, carefully cut a small V-shape at opposite sides of the rim of the cup. Don't go too heavy with the scissors in case you split the cup down the side. Balance a pencil across the V-shapes and tie the wick round the pencil in the middle, pulling so that the wick is taut.

Heat the candle in a container balanced in a few centimeters of water in a pan on the hob. As they often come in glass jars, you only need to pop that in the pan, making sure the water doesn't come more than halfway up the side of the jar. Once the wax is all melted, skim out any bits that may have dropped in, including the old wick and its weight.

Allow the wax to cool slightly – it should start clouding over and making a slight 'skin' on the top, before pouring it gently into the plastic cup. It shouldn't be scalding hot, or the plastic will melt, but you might want to protect your hands with a teatowel.

Leave to set overnight and then gently warm the outside of the cup (by submerging it in a pot of boiling water briefly) until the candle comes away on the inside. Place on a flameproof plate or bowl and light to enjoy once more. If you have lots of smelly bits left over, try layering one on top of the other. Let each smelly layer set first and chill it in the fridge so that the next hot layer doesn't mix with the one below.

Chapter Three

Some stuff to play with

t must be a universal truth that all parents are really horrid and selfish and determined to make their kids' lives a misery. Well, we must be because every other day there's a plaintive wail from the bedroom: 'But I've got *no* toys to play with!' It's a miracle that Messrs Argos and Toys R Us have ever made any money with this nation of scrooges.

Rather than rushing out to the shops to atone for such parental misdeeds, stop and have a look around. It's possible that you have the wherewithal for some decent games knocking around the house. And the benefits of getting kids to make their own toys are almost limitless.

First, making toys takes them hours of quiet concentration (i.e. more gin time for you). Then, they have the satisfaction of playing with something made by their own fair hands. And when they, inevitably, bore of it and leave it to moulder in the corner, you can break it up into its constituent parts, binning or putting it away as you see fit. You are safe in the knowledge that you're not binning yet more twenty-quid bits of violently lime-green plastic that's toxic both to the environment and your design ethic.

Poi

This is essentially a tennis ball on a piece of string, but a poi sounds better. For a fairly simple concept, these swinging bits of ribbon make a fairly impressive display. The effect is a bit like those gymnasts who run around a blue mat with long bits of ribbon that frequently cause pot-bellied middle-aged men to claim: '*Pffft!* I could do that.' Now's their chance to prove it.

1 Take two tennis balls, squash balls or small bean bags. Golf balls will give the same effect but are a damn sight more painful if you get the moves wrong.

2 Poke a hole through the tennis ball with a sharp knitting needle or skewer. Through this, thread one end of a bit of string. How long is a piece of string? In this case as long as the swinger of the poi, or at least as long as the distance between their wrists and the floor when they've got their arms loosely by their sides. Minus 15cm. See, it's very exact.

3 When the string is threaded through, tie a knot in the end. You may want to make a 'washer' out of a bit of tough plastic, which stops the knot eventually working its way into the hole from the centrifugal force and sending your tennis ball through the neighbour's window at some considerable velocity when you least expect it.

4 Make a small loop in the other end of the string and thread some nice, soft but not stretchy cloth to make a handle big enough for you to comfortably put your hands through.

5 Now it's time to get creative. At the simplest, you can glue some thin tapering bits of bright cloth or wideish ribbon around a metre long to the end of the tennis ball. Or you can attach some floaty brightly coloured chiffon to the length of the string. Or, you can ... experiment.

The way to play with a poi is really quite simple. Standing up, take a poi in each hand and swing it round in a circle. You don't need to be frantic, gentle circles will do. Try spinning one in one direction, and one the other. Then do it in front instead of beside you. Then above your head. Then under one leg. Then wherever you can without dinging yourself or your neighbours in the head.

Tents/Explorers

This is a good game for one person or more, both indoors and out. Most of the fun to be honest is in the setting up because afterwards what do you do? Sit in a tent? There's plenty of time to practise that on wet camping holidays in Dorset.

Let the kids have a grotty sheet that you don't need anymore. For indoors, drape it over the back of two or three dining chairs. Outside hang it tepee style from a low branch. Proper explorers need lots of equipment so they need to prepare tinned food, maps, warm clothing and anything else for an epic voyage to the rockery.

Of course, this is all on the understanding that they put it all back when they've finally discovered the south pole/America/the garden shed.

Elastics

This is a very simple game that demonstrated to me my complete lack of gymnastic ability.

You need at least three players, and a lot of elastic bands. Link the bands together in a long rope until it reaches 2–3 metres when pulled straight, but not taut – it's going to get some more serious bending so you need to make sure it doesn't sag but has plenty of 'give'.

Two people hold each end of the elastic at a nominated point on the body, starting with the toes. The runner then takes a run up and jumps over the elastic. It doesn't take much imagination to see that falling over the elastic at toe height would be humiliating but unlikely. At head height, it's no less embarrassing, but has a great deal more potential to happen.

The runner keeps jumping over the elastic as it gets moved higher and higher (from toes to ankles to knees and so on) until they can't make it over first time. They have two 'jokers' where they can get away with having someone stand on the elastic to give them a 'V' to jump through, or they can use their own hand to push it down while they jump. Even with these aids, however, at no point can your feet 'clip' the elastic on the way over. On failing, you take one end of the elastic, and the person you've relieved starts their turn.

Thaumotrope

This is a basic form of animation and much easier to knock up than its cousin the zoetrope (see right).

Cut a circle from a piece of thin cardboard (hello, cereal box!). Draw a picture of a head with an apple on the top. We're not looking for Van Gogh here. A smiley face will do if you're really artistically challenged. Cut another piece of cardboard exactly the same size and draw an arrow on it. Stick a straw, or a straight stick, or chopstick to the back of the cardboard with the head on it, pointing north–south. Then stick the back of the piece with the arrow to the other side of the straw and face/cardboard so it

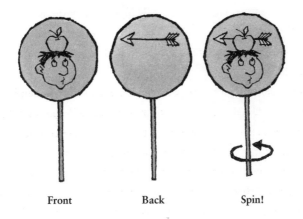

Front	Back	Spin!

makes one circle with a straw going through the middle. Put the bottom end of the straw between the palms of your hands and rub them together quickly, spinning the cardboard to and fro. The two images will merge and you have the beginnings of your own cartoon. Hold the phone, Mr Disney, I'm a-comin'!

Zoetrope

So, single-frame animation just doesn't cut the mustard, eh? You want a film that actually lasts, ooh, seconds? That'll be your zoetrope then.

These were popular in Victorian times and often featured at 'end of the pier shows' where for a groat or a penny, or whatever it was they had then, dirty old men tired of looking at table legs got their jollies on 'What the butler saw' wind-up machines.

To make a zoetrope, you need to construct a small drum-shaped object. Take a pencil that's fairly new, i.e. still longish, and, ideally, has a big, useless eraser on the end. Cut a circle about the size of a small pizza (15cm diameter) from some very stiff card (goodbye, cereal box, hello, packing box!). Using a drawing pin, attach the circle to the eraser end of the pencil through the centre point.

Wrap some stiff paper all the way round the edge of the cardboard circle to see how much you'll need. You could do some fancy sums with pi but this

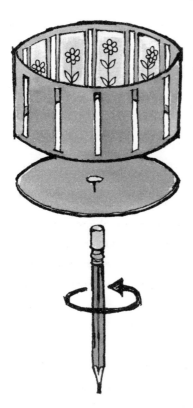

is quicker. Lay the paper out flat and create your animation frames.

Each frame needs to be a simple progression from the one before, so that the difference can be seen clearly. Take a skipping girl, for example. It should take about four frames for her skipping rope to go from above her head to under her feet. At the same time, she'll be rising off the floor to reach the highest point of her skip by the fourth frame. Then ditto for her coming back down again. Spread the frames out evenly along the paper, and, in between each frame, you need to cut a small, rectangular window, no thicker than your index finger and only slightly longer than the pictures.

When you've drawn your pictures and cut out your windows, fold the paper round the edge of the cardboard circle again and fix with glue or sellotape. That's your zoetrope complete and all you have to do to make it work is to spin it round. If the pin is too snug against the cardboard circle, you might want to tease it out so that the 'drum' spins more freely. The world will spin, the girl will skip about and everyone can feel very smug for inventing telly.

Splat the rat

A very simple game of reflexes where part of the fun for mums is getting the kids to spend a goodish chunk of time making the equipment on their own in the first place.

You'll need to make some 'rats', which are simple bean bags made

from old socks (make sure there aren't any holes, otherwise you'll end up with exploding rats, prematurely terminating the game). Fill the feet with rice, lentils or small pasta shapes and secure the end so that nothing leaks out, even under pressure. You can tie an elastic band round the end very, very tightly or a more permanent solution is to stitch the ends closed. Decorate to make as rat-like as desired.

Find a tube wide enough for the rat to be able to slide down unimpeded but unseen by the contenders. A spare piece of plastic pipe or guttering does the job well. The key word here is 'spare'.

The gamesmaster takes charge of one end of the tube and the supply of rats. The player stands at the other end with a 'splatting' implement, such as a hockey stick, old cricket bat or just a sturdy pole. About a foot beyond the player's end of the tube is a marker or line. The distance between the end of the tube and the line is the maximum splatting area. If the rat makes it past the line without being splatted it is 'safe'.

The gamesmaster then raises the pole up to a nice steep angle (for maximum rat speed) – shorter masters may want to stand on a chair for this one. They then throw rats down the tube in quick succession, the splatter having to 'splat' them as soon as they shoot out the other end. Points are scored for the number of rats splatted. You can make it more difficult by varying the size of the rats, 'baby' rats being the hardest to splat.

Everyone takes turns to splat and the highest scoring splatter wins. If you ever have to 'volunteer' to run a fund-raising stall at a school fête or similar horror, this is a good, low-maintenance game to look after. Charge a pound a go and the highest scorer overall wins a collection of soft toys. (Yes, the rats.)

Buzzin' balloons

If you gather enough materials together you can have some fairly impressive races down the garden path with these. Just make sure each competitor has a different coloured balloon.

This game/toy makes great use of those DVDs of straight-to-TV films

you never wanted to watch that come with newspapers and magazines.

Unscrew the pop-up spout from one of those 'sports' bottles and glue the base over the hole in the centre of the CD. Use any type of glue you like – even some sellotape would do – but make sure it is completely airtight. Close the spout (for the time being). Blow up the balloon but don't tie it shut. Holding it closed with your fingers, stretch the spare rubber at the end over the spout.

Line up the balloons on the start line, and, with your fingers still preventing air from escaping from the balloon, use your other hand to open the spout inside the balloon. Let the balloon go and watch it hover off down the path/round the room on a blanket of air. When you run out of air, just pop the balloon round to the filling station (your lungs, via your mouth) and fill it up again.

Top tip: There are only so many balloon hovercraft a person can make. Give the kids all the leftover CDs and send them into the garden. Get them to make multi-CD mobiles with twigs and string and dangle around succulent seedlings and re-sown grass to scare off birds. You can also smash them into sharp shards and scatter them around plants to deter slugs, as well as cats that dig around your petunias for a suitable place to take a pee.

Orchestral manoeuvres

Line up eight glasses (not your best crystal) of about the same size and shape. Fill the first glass about ⅛th full of water for the high note, the second glass should be ¼ full, the third glass should be ⅜ths full for the next note, and so on. Each glass should sound like a note on the music scale (doh, ray, mi, fah, soh, lah, ti, doh).

You may need to tune your 'instruments' by removing or adding water a teaspoon at a time. Then, using a metal teaspoon, gently tap the tops of the glasses to make sweet, sweet music. Customise the instruments by using a different food colouring (just a couple of drops should do it) for each note.

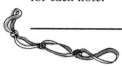

It takes a bit of practice but you can reproduce the sounds by running a damp finger round the rim of each glass until the vibrations make the notes sing out. Because it takes a while to make each note, it's not the best method for an instantly rousing rendition of 'Doe, a deer ...'.

Parachuting soldiers

For some reason, toy soldiers and Polly Pocket-type figurines hold endless fascination for kids, but after so many hand-to-hand combats and demure tea parties (I'll leave it up to you to decide which is which) it all gets a bit boring. After all, they don't really *do* much. But, with a simple hanky and some string, suddenly, your infantry is airborne providing, ooh, minutes of pleasure. Cut a length of string into four equal pieces about 50cm long. Tie one to each corner of the hankie, then tie them all together and fix to the figurine. Find something high, like a staircase, and throw them off.

Silly slime

Kids love nothing better than stuff that goes squelch or splat. This is great just for the hell of it because it's so easy to make and mess around with, but it's also a handy accessory for any gross-out plans at Halloween.

Mix 1 cup of cornflour with 1 cup of water. Use your hands to mix it until it is a smooth texture. You can make it thicker and gooier by adding a second cup of cornflour. Kids love adding food colouring or paint to make it even more gruesome.

Provided you don't mind staining the clothing (food colouring is nearly impossible to get out of fabric) you could try this trick: fill a plastic freezer bag with green-coloured silly slime and drip some red colouring around it once it's in the bag – don't try to mix it in, you want it to come out all streaky.

Tie the bag tightly so that the contents are secure and the bag is strained. Attach it with some thread (choose one that's difficult to spot) to a shirt button at roughly stomach level. When a suitable time comes you need to get an implement that's sharp enough to puncture the bag but not enough to puncture you too. A cocktail stick is good. Make a gap in the shirt where the bag is, and 'stab' yourself with the stick. Squeeze both hands to your middle while groaning and writhing and peek through half-closed eyes at horrified faces witnessing what appears to be green and red ectoplasm leaking from your 'wound'.

If you're feeling very adventurous, you can make some with an eggy-yellow tinge and put small dollops onto cling film and twist the ends. Glue it to your forehead with some Pritt Stick and watch as people go green when you burst your 'pustules' in their face.

Steady Eddie

This is a simple buzzer game to test steady hands, and you can make it as easy or as difficult as you like. You can even change the level of challenge mid-game. The idea is to trace a metal hoop along a metal wire without their touching each other. If you do – *BZZZT!* You lose!

You need to get hold of an all-wire, unwound coathanger with the hook cut off. Also, find a battery-operated doorbell that uses less than 24 volts. Whatever you do, don't pinch one off the door that's wired to the mains. You really, really don't want to find out what happens when you go poking wire coathangers into the National Grid.

Get a block of wood to use as the base for your game. Length and width is up to you, but it'll be determined by how long your coathanger is when you stretch it out, and how many kinks you want to put in it (more, deeper kinks = harder game). Drill two deep, thin holes wide enough to slot the ends of coathanger into.

If you take the button out of the middle of your doorbell, there should be two wires. Touch them together – they'll make the bell buzz. Take one of the doorbell wires and tape it to one end of the coathanger, near the wood, making sure the two metals touch.

Tape the other doorbell wire to the coathanger hook that you cut off earlier. Bend the hook round the coathanger 'trail' so it makes a closed hoop. Wrap a bit more tape round the other end of the coathanger near the wood. Having both ends wound in tape means that when you rest the hook down it won't be constantly buzzing.

Between you and me, once the kids have gone to bed this turns into an excellent drinking game. And like all good drinking games, the more mistakes you make, the more mistakes you make!

Games

Kit's game

I don't know why this is called Kit's game; it could just as easily be called Jeremy's game. But it's a very easy game and any number of people can play. Just gather together a collection of household objects: keys, wooden spoon, egg cup – that sort of thing. Spread them out on a tray, or a small table top. You don't want more than can be covered with a tea towel.

Give the players a minute to memorise all the items on the tray, then cover it up again with the tea towel. Remove one item from under the tea towel as silently as possible so they don't guess what it is (rattling your keys under the table is a bit of a giveaway) then reveal the tray again. The first person to figure out what is missing wins. You can do it again and again, removing something different each time, until everyone gets bored or you run out of things to hide.

Cat's cradle

In cat's cradle, two people make shapes with string and pass them back and forth. Lots of people know the *first* one (the cat's cradle) – but there are lots more: the manger, candles, the cat's eye and diamonds … it goes on and on. To do it, you need two people – one to hold the string steady, the other to do the 'picking and weaving' and a piece of string tied at the ends to make a circle.

Put your hands through the string. Keep your thumb out of it. Wrap the string around each hand. Keep your thumb out of the loop. Put the middle finger of one hand through the loop on the other hand and pull. Put the middle finger of the other hand through the loop. This is the cat's cradle. But any old person can do that. Here are some trickier moves.

Find the two places where the string makes an X. While you're still holding the cat's cradle, the other person takes their thumb and forefinger

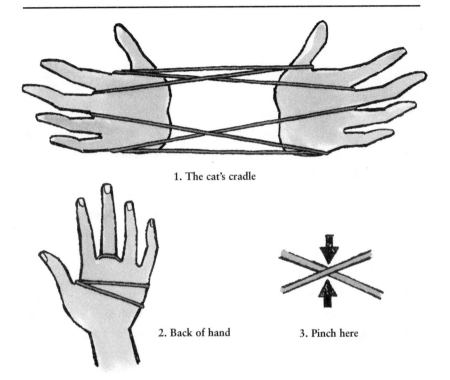

1. The cat's cradle

2. Back of hand   3. Pinch here

and pinches those X-shaped parts. Still pinching them, they move their hands further apart, until the string is tight. They then point their fingers down the sides and then bring them up through the middle pulling gently. As that happens, let the cat's cradle slide out of your hands. That's how to transfer it across.

Now you pinch the Xs from the top, not the sides. Holding onto them, pull your hands apart, and then push in towards the middle, still holding the Xs. Bring your fingers back up through the middle and then pull them apart again. Now you have what are called tramlines or candles.

Using opposing pinkies, that is, with the right little finger pull the left top string all the way over to the right, beyond the outside strings. With the left little finger, pull the right top string to the left. Now there are two little triangles. Holding the ends of the triangles tightly in the pinkies – it's a bit tricky – turn the hands and dip under with thumb and forefinger.

Then, still holding on tightly with the pinkies, push the thumbs and forefingers up through the middle. Still holding onto the bottom string tightly with pinkies, spread the thumbs and index fingers while the other person lets go. And if you're not currently wrapped up in lots of knots you should have a shape called the manger!

But you can go still further. Pinch the X-shapes you've made with thumb and forefinger. Still pinching the Xs, pull them out. Now, pull them up a little and then turn your hands over and pinching tightly, pointing your thumb and forefinger down, dive down into the middle. Spread your thumb and forefinger apart, still pointing down, and you have diamonds.

Card games

Simple to play, eminently portable and no upper age limit makes a game of cards a guaranteed crowd pleaser. Knowing the rules to even just two or three games helps. Invariably, as with Scrabble, the biggest arguments with card games begin when players have different versions of the rules. For argument's sake, this is the definitive way of playing these card games and that's THAT.

Snap

Divide the pack of cards equally among the players. Decide who goes first (left of the dealer is the usual) and that person turns over the first card. Keep going until someone puts down a card that matches the one before (e.g. a jack on a jack) then it's the first person to slam their hand down on the pack of cards and shout 'snap' who wins. They get to keep all the cards that have been put down so far. The game keeps going until one player ends up with all of the cards. Remember, it's not the person who puts the matching card down who claims 'Snap!', it's just whoever gets their hand down first.

Blackjack

Possibly the most over-used game name in cards. It can be a version of Pontoon, or 21, as it's played in casinos. My version is a bit longer and a bit more vicious towards your fellow players. Which is always fun.

Deal each player seven cards. Put the remainder of the pack face down in a stack and turn over the top card. Each player then puts a card down following the suit or the number, i.e. 7 of spades can be followed by another 7 or a spade. If you can't match the card, you pick up a card from the stack instead. The winner is the one who has no cards left. Simple enough.

However, there are a number of forfeits that prolong the agony:

Black Jack: if a player puts down a black jack, the next player along picks up five cards from the stack, unless …

Double Black Jack: they have a black jack too, and put it down, making the next player along pick up ten cards from the stack, unless …

Red Jack: if they put down a red jack this cancels out the black jack forfeit and play simply moves on.

Two: If the preceding player puts down a 2, the next in line picks up two cards from the stack. However, if they also have a 2, they can put it down and make the next player pick up four. This can go on all the way up to picking up eight cards.

Eight: If you put down an 8, the player on your left (play always goes to the left) misses a go.

Ace: You can use an ace to change the suit being played, but remember that if you play it to change to hearts, for example, you've got to wait until your next turn before you can play a heart. If lots of people are playing, the suit may well be changed before it gets round to you again.

Last card: If a player puts down their second-to-last card, they are one go away from winning the game. As they put this card down, they must shout 'Last card' before their turn is over. If they fail to do so and another player notices once play has moved on, they must pick up another card as a penalty. They don't miss their next go though.

Rummy

This is one of the first games my grandma taught me. It's simple enough for quite young kids to play but still makes adults pretty competitive.

Deal each player seven cards and leave the remaining stack with one turned over again. Each player takes turns to pick up a card and discard a less useful one. You are aiming to make a 'run' and/or three of a kind (you can have four if you're very smart).

A run is consecutive cards in one suit – jack, queen, king of hearts, for example. A run must be at least three long but can be all seven cards if you want. Ace is either one or tops off the king – it can be both in this game.

Keep picking up and putting down cards until you have your runs etc. Some are confident and like to put the whole hand down in a flourish in one go.

Whist

You start whist by dealing each person a hand of seven cards. The player to the left of the dealer cuts the pack to determine a 'trump', i.e. hearts. This means that whatever went before can be cancelled by a trump card, unless of course it is also a trump card (more of which later).

Then each player takes their turn to put down a card. The next player must try to beat the value of that card (e.g. an 8 of clubs beats a 5 of clubs), and the next player must try to beat that and so on until every player has had a turn. The player who put down the highest value card wins the round and keeps the pile of cards. If a player cannot put down a card of the same suit, they either a) throw in a useless card guaranteeing they can't win the pile or b) throw in a trump card to win that round. The trump card can be numerically lower than any of the cards there. It wins simply by being in the trump suit. However, a higher value trump can beat it (e.g. 6 of hearts will beat 2 of hearts). When all players have thrown one card into the pile, the winner gathers them up and they start the next round.

Play continues until all the cards have been played, and the winner of

the round is the one with the most piles of cards. In the next round, six cards are dealt, and then five cards after that. On the final round, each player has only one card each and whoever puts down the highest value card, wins.

Patience

To set the game up, lay out a row of seven cards, all face down except the first one. Then, in an overlapping row below, add a row of six cards with the first one face up. Continue adding rows in this manner until there is only one card left in the final row (as shown).

The aim of patience is to create runs down each column of cards in alternative colours and descending numbers, such as black 10, red 9, black 8 etc. You deal out the remaining cards, uncovering every third one, and add to the columns where appropriate. When sequences start to appear, you can move them together to make longer runs. Uncover the remaining card and see if that fits anywhere too. You may move a card or a sequence here to free up more face-down cards but it must begin with a face card: king, queen or jack. This tableau changes as the game progresses so keep an eye out for opportunities to reveal more face-down cards.

Finally, if you turn over an ace, such as the ace of spades, you may begin a 'suit pile' by placing the ace to the side. Once the next suitable card

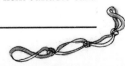

becomes available, i.e. 2 of spades, you can put it on top of the ace. You can only move cards to the suit piles if they are 'free', i.e. at the bottom of a sequence, the first card in a sequence with no others following it or the top card of the set of three that you count out from the pile of spares.

Moving to the suit piles is also the way to get the game 'out' – to win. If all the suit piles are full then inevitably there are no cards left on the table or in the spares pile. However, because you can only move 'free' cards to the pile, and some are trapped in a sequence where the lower cards cannot be moved because they have no ace to go to yet, it is still possible to lose as the game will not go out. This is why it's called patience. It would try a saint's, as you count past the card you need to get out for the fifth time and still can't get at it because it's underneath the useless top card. So near and yet so far.

Cheating? It's considered cheating if you pay the cards out from the spares pile one at a time rather than three at a time, and it is also simply 'not done' to fill an empty space with anything other than a face card. But if you do use either, or both, of these methods, it is still possible to lose as the essential cards you need to complete a sequence, fill a gap or start a suit pile may remain trapped face down on the table under an immovable sequence.

Sounds complicated, but isn't really and the game is just frustrating enough to want to keep 'having a go' for hours. The question is: Have you had the patience to finish all these instructions? Aw, just have a go, you'll see what I mean!

Pelminism

This is just an easy, old-fashioned memory game. Lay out the entire pack of cards face down in a grid. Each player takes turns to turn over two cards. They then try to remember where these cards were for when their turn comes round again. The idea is to find a pair, which the player then keeps. If a player finds a pair, they can go again and keep playing until they fail to find a match. The game continues until all pairs are found and the winner is the one who has collected most pairs. Pairs are taken at face value so a 2 matches a 2 and a queen a queen, regardless of what suit they are in. If you want a quicker game, reduce the size of the pack to just the reds or the blacks. Don't just cut the pack in half. There will be hardly any pairs and you'll go on for ever before you realise that it's impossible to win.

House of cards

All you need is a stable table-top, a pack of cards, an absence of wind or troublemakers and a steady hand. Simply place the cards in pyramids, end to end in a row until you have about seven pyramids. Gently (oh, ever so gently), place a 'floor' of slightly overlapping cards between the pyramid peaks. Then, begin building (ever, ever so gently) another row of pyramids (five or so) on that level. Repeat until you've run out of cards or patience after it's fallen down for the fiftieth time.

Chapter Four

Some stretchy stuff

12 things to do with a pair of tights

1 Wigmaking
2 Silly snake draught excluder
3 Soft toy stuffing
4 Making scarecrows
5 Straining jam
6 Bean bags
7 Swingball
8 Growing plants
9 Bug jars
10 Robbing banks
11 Feeley tights
12 Central heating

Tights are handy in all sorts of ways. Just wearing them can stop you getting bitten by carnivorous bugs. If you slip one over the end of your vacuum cleaner, you can use it to find and pick up small bits of lost jewellery and stray contact lenses. And you can use them to repair cars when the fan belt goes, letting you limp on 20 miles or so to the nearest garage.

While it would be economical to use old, laddered tights for many of the following suggestions, you might want to use a brand-new pair for activities that involve putting your head in them. No matter how fresh and fragrant you are, some people refuse to stick their head in an old pair of tights.

Wigmaking

Cut the legs off the tights and sew up the holes left on the delightfully termed 'gusset' part. Using a large-holed needle, thread the required length of wool, ribbon or string through for 'hair'. Don't knot the ends. Sew from the inside out, pulling the thread until it's almost all the way through. Make one small stitch in the tights then cut the thread in half right next to the needle. Obviously, the thicker the wool or string, the faster you'll be finished.

When the wig is as full as you'd like, you can give it a trim to even off the ends – just remember that if you cut it too short, it won't grow back! If you want your wig to be the same length all over (good for Egyptian costumes), you should use longer lengths of wool the nearer to the crown you get.

For curly hair, use paper-based ribbon and use a knife or pair of scissors to get the curl. Using the sharp edge – carefully – lay the ribbon across the blade, holding the end with your other hand. Place the thumb of the hand holding the blade carefully but firmly over the ribbon and pull away firmly. You should get a springy curl. If it's not curly enough, you can repeat the process more firmly but after a few attempts the ribbon will lose its curlability.

Silly snake draught excluder

Chop a leg off the tights and stuff it with chopped-up bits of old tights, T-shirts and jumpers. You could leave it like that but it would look a bit like someone had left their large intestine hanging around under your front door. How about decorating it?

You could give it some fur (in a Mum Stuff world, snakes can have fur) by using the wig method above. You could wrap it in cloth, or ribbon. Use a few twists of black, yellow and red to make a coral snake. Brown cloth makes a good sausage dog body. Green cloth with bits of silver ribbon sticking out here and there and you've got a caterpillar (wind some string or even elastic bands at intervals down its body for the genuine lumpy caterpillar effect). Buttons for eyes, ribbon for tongues and wool for hair are all good accessories.

Soft toy stuffing

Chopped tights make the best homemade stuffing because they aren't at all lumpy and will fit any shape. Nude or black tights are good for stuffing knitted toys because they don't show through the gaps in the knit.

They are also handy for repairs to teddies that have had the stuffing quite literally knocked out of them. Chop a pair of tights into 2–3in sections (you don't need to be terribly precise) and stuff through the offending hole.

Making scarecrows

Two pairs of stuffed tights make a great scarecrow body. Simply stuff them both full, twisting the ends and tie a knot a little way up to make feet and hands. When both pairs are stuffed as full as they'll go, sew the tops of each pair together to make the body.

Use the gusset of another pair to make the head, remembering to sew up the chopped-off leg holes, or all of scarecrow's brains will fall out. If you want Mr Crow to have a full head of hair, sew on a wig (see page 66), before you stuff it. However, it's probably quicker to stick some lengths of wool to the inside of an old hat. Again, buttons make great eyes but it's equally simple just to cut out shapes from cardboard and glue them on. Traditionally, scarecrows are stuffed with hay, so for authenticity, you might want to have some strands of hay sticking out of your scarecrow's clothing and shoes.

For a bit of a festive twist, dress your scarecrow up in a Santa outfit and send dad up a ladder to hang him off the chimney.

Straining jam

Once you've finished scouring the countryside for edibles (see Chapter Six), a pair of tights comes in very handy for getting the inedible bits of the countryside out of your blackberry jam, or rosehip syrup. Probably best not to reveal this to the kids though. They might have a hard time deciding what's worse – that you've spent the last 10 minutes extracting boiled spiders from their morning spread, or that you did it using your sweaty tights.

Bean bags

Particularly with young children around, it's always handy to have some soft things to throw around. Cut off the legs of the tights and then cut into 50cm sections. Tie a knot tightly in one end of the section and fill with small, bean-like contents. Small pulses such as split peas, lentils, couscous or bulgur wheat work well. Fill until the stocking is full but not jam-packed. You don't want to throw it and find it explodes everywhere on impact. To have different coloured bean bags, use an ordinary cloth dye like Dylon, or try out one of the home-made dyes (see page 26). Alternatively, use different coloured tights!

Swingball

Cut a leg off a pair of tights and drop a tennis ball into the foot. Tie the top end tightly to the top of any available pole, i.e. the middle of a rotary washing line. Take one child with energy to burn, one tennis racket and leave them in the garden to whack it round and round in circles.

Growing plants

This is great if you don't have a lot of garden space to give over to budding gardeners. Fill both legs of the tights with earth – you don't need to buy expensive compost, top soil from your borders is fine. Make sure you take out any sharp stones or bits of glass first as you don't want the legs splitting all over the kitchen floor. Also, don't fill it full to bursting. Cut little holes at 50cm intervals and plant any kid-friendly seeds – tomatoes, cucumbers and lettuce grow quickly and give easy crops. Simple little flowers are also quite rewarding. Put it somewhere that gets light and air and isn't too cold or too hot and leave to grow.

Bug jars

Lots of kids are quite rightly fascinated by everything creepy and crawly. There's nothing they enjoy more than grubbing around in the dirt and re-homing some unsuspecting stick insect. Budding zoologists do have a basic grasp of biology and are aware that insect + no air = dead insect. To promote the humane capture of various wrigglies, provide the kids with a nice big jar and a pair of tights that they can secure over the top. Escape proof and thoroughly fresh-air friendly.

Robbing banks

Pulling a pair of tights over your head and shouting 'stick 'em up' in the local Halifax is not advisable. But at home, it's good fun for making silly faces.

Feely tights

A good instant game that can be played competitively, or just for fun. Provided you're careful and don't use anything outrageous like a sea urchin, for example, you also have a good chance of finishing the game with your tights intact.

Using opaque or woolly tights, stick a few household objects down the legs. Each player gets a leg. They have to stick their hand down the leg and guess what each item is before pulling it out to have a look. They put the objects in a pile of 'got right' and 'not right'. The winner has the biggest pile of got rights. If you're just playing with one child, the number of got rights corresponds with the number of sweetie rewards.

Central heating

You can also use tights to keep warm – regardless of what sex you are. It's a well-known fact that big, hairy beer-drinking blokes who work outside during the winter months pinch their wives' 40 deniers on a regular basis. However, this does not mean you should send your short-trousered 10-year-old to school in a nice pair of champagne nylons on a nippy morning.

Chapter Five

Some food stuff

T he only recipe previous generations of men and kids needed
was: Find kitchen. Insert mother. Mix with shopping and leave
to marinate for one hour. After dinner, retire to living room
while magic pixies do the washing up.

Today, not much has changed. I go shopping (for shoes) and I spend hours
in the kitchen. Except, instead of being found chained to the oven door, I'm
more likely to be perched at the breakfast bar, gin in one hand, telly remote in
the other, enjoying blissful refuge from the train-set-related chaos currently
dominating the living room. The dinner will of course be well under control
and I estimate the local Indian takeaway will be delivering in 3 … 2 … 1 …

But the kitchen needn't be viewed as a culinary prison. Don't tell
anyone, but the kitchen holds a whole arsenal of fun stuff to make, bake
and blow up. When you manage to blow up 2 litres of Diet Coke, a bunch
of grapes and a tub of baking soda, you'll really see what I mean.

Dishing the dirt

Food doesn't just magic itself out of nowhere. I know that it mostly comes
from Mr Sainsbury, but even he has to find it from somewhere. And that
somewhere is usually the ground. So let's start our culinary adventures
right back at the beginning. Now, even the least green-fingered child can
tell you that you need four magic ingredients to make food grow: seed, soil,
water and sun.

Rubbish. To grow an avocado, you need string but no soil. To grow a pineapple, you need a plate but no seeds. To grow cress, you need water, light and cotton wool but no soil. And to grow everything below, you don't even need a garden. The kitchen shelf will do just fine.

Cressed out

Take your sock/cotton wool/whatever, dampen it and leave it somewhere warm, dry and bright, but not in direct sunlight or it'll just dry out completely and scorch. Sprinkle seeds evenly across the top and go away. Come back now and again to check that it's still dampish, and give it a light mist of water if it looks as if it's drying out. Cut to a week later ...

Cress! Harvest with a pair of scissors and stick in your eggy sandwich.

The avocado in a jar mystery

Many gardeners begin their avocado plants by piercing the seed with toothpicks and then suspending it (pointed end up) over a glass, vase, or jar of water. In two to six weeks, if the seed germinates, you should have a young plant, ready to pot. However, not all avocado seeds will germinate in this way. If your seed hasn't sprouted in six weeks, toss it out and try again.

More conventionally, you can leave the stone in the sunlight until it begins to split and then pot it in soil partly exposed. Use a 4- or 5-inch pot to start your plant and set it in a nutrient-rich potting soil that has good drainage. After your plant is about a foot tall, pinch it back to half. Pinching it back produces a rounder and fuller plant. Once your plant has filled its pot with roots, it's time to move it to its permanent home.

Pineapples from a cold climate

Everyone knows that pineapples come from the hot, tropical countries in holiday brochures. Trying to grow one in wet, cold, grey Blighty is about as easy as nailing jelly to the wall. Well, it is if your try to do it outside, where it's cold. Do it where it is warm – on top of the fridge – and you'll get a whole different result.

Cut off the top of the pineapple, about 2in below the leaves, so that the surface is level and flat, with no jagged edges. Remove some, but not all, of the leaves and let the pineapple top dry out for a few days before 'planting' it.

Place your pineapple top in a shallow dish (about 2in deep) that has some holes for drainage in the bottom. You might want to put some kitchen towel below it. Fill the dish with vermiculite (from the garden centre) almost to the top and then push the pineapple top about an inch into it. Lightly moisten the vermiculite. You don't want it soggy or the pineapple will rot. Pop it on top of the fridge in the path of some natural light and wait for new green leaves to grow.

If it seems to be a very dry atmosphere, put a plastic bag over the top to keep the moisture in, and take it off when you see the green shoots. This should take about three weeks. Once you've got your green shoots, you can replant it in 'real' soil in a 'real' pot, but bearing in mind our climate, you'll probably have to keep it indoors. The likelihood of a pineapple tree growing fruit with this method is low, but it's fun trying.

Tread gingerly

Pierce a 2in-long piece of ginger at one end with toothpicks. Balance the toothpicks across the rim of a glass, with the ginger dangling down inside. Fill with water until the bottom third of it is submerged. When roots are 1in long, plant in soil just below the surface. Place in natural light, but not direct sunlight. Small stems and leaves will appear.

Worm compost

Wormeries are little colonies of worms that sit in a darkened box and chomp their way happily through your potato peelings, apple cores and leftover broccoli. You can even chuck in egg shells because despite having no discernible teeth or bones, like all little critters they need their calcium. The stuff they then, ahem, excrete is vastly reduced in size and full of yummy nutrients that your tomatoes will just *love*.

All they need is a nice dark box (a wooden crate with no gaps or an old fishtank will do) in a nice quiet place that you top up with leftovers from time to time.

To get hold of your worms, you can simply go and dig them up out of the ground. But if you don't have a handy back garden, or after some experimentation your garden just isn't 'wormy' enough, tiger worms from a fishing tackle shop are a good bet, and they cost hardly anything.

Simply tear up some paper and mix it with some moss (find an old wall or bunch of old stones and scrape it off). Worms like the damp so damp the mix down but not so it turns to sludge. Add a thick layer of vegetable matter, that's the old peelings etc. and then another layer of damp newspaper/moss stuff. Then bung in the worms and cover with a lid that has some cracks or holes in it to let the air in.

It takes about three months before your worms will have made enough compost to reuse in the garden but in the meantime you can just enjoy watching them wiggle around, make worm babies and just have a nice, wormy time of it. To make sure you don't evict half of your colony along with the compost, shine a bright light onto the box or tub (this is why having a see-through tub like a fishtank makes life easier) and they should all wiggle down to the bottom out of the way. Worms don't like light, which is why you should keep your viewing times to a minimum.

And then it went 'boom'!

Mums, eh? There we are, standing innocently by in our pinnies with a grape in one hand and a microwave in the other. What mischief could we possibly get up to?

Dads may think they've got the monopoly on things that fizz, whiz and bang, but confront them with a fan oven and they're lost. As mums, we've got the technology and we know how to use it. And using it for a Victoria sponge cake is just the tip of the iceberg. Shakespeare chose three witches, a cauldron and some eye of newt. I only need a bottle of cola and some minty sweets for all hell to break loose.

The Coke fountain

I know as mums we're supposed to discourage all forms of drink spillage, food playfulness and assorted mucky pursuits, but some things are just too much fun to pass up. If the kids ever, ever suggest that mums are in the tiniest way boring, this is a great trick to pull. It takes seconds to set up, the results are frankly mind-blowing, and they'll never look at you in the same light again.

March the kids (and Dad, it'll blow his mind too) outside to somewhere you don't mind getting covered in fizzy pop. Bring with you: one 2-litre bottle of Diet Coke and one normal size pack of Mentos mint sweets.

Place the bottle upright and full on some steady, flat ground. Open the bottle. Open the pack of Mentos so that they're all still lined up, but will tip out of your hand in one smooth column when upended. Tip Mentos through neck of cola bottle all at once.

Run away.

Observe five-foot fountain of Diet Coke that is now gushing from the bottle and covering your assembled family. Smile, say nothing and return to whatever you were doing, leaving family to marvel at this hitherto undiscovered side of complete madness, and wondering if you have a secret sideline as an MI5 operative.

An important health and safety point: You will not explode if you eat a packet of Mentos then drink Diet Coke. You will probably burp.

Foam blasters

These foam blasters are thoroughly messy and stain everything in sight. You have been warned.

Get hold of enough empty 2-litre fizzy pop bottles for everyone involved. You should have plenty left after the Diet Coke drama. Fill it almost to the top with warm (not hot) water, and add a squirt of washing-up liquid.

Gather the ammunition: A bottle of vinegar (any cheap stuff will do, preferably not balsamic), some pots of baking soda and food colouring.

Add a couple of tablespoons of baking soda to the water. Put your hand over the top and give it a good shake to get a 'head' of bubbles. Drip some food colouring onto the bubbles. Pour in some vinegar. There's no specific amount, but it's not a lot as the action begins pretty much straight away. Point at your opponent and let the foam fight commence!

If your foam runs out, just chuck in a bit more baking soda and vinegar and the whole thing will keep going.

DON'T SCREW THE CAP BACK ON. IT WILL EXPLODE!!
DON'T DRINK THE MIXTURE!!
DON'T THINK THE STAINS WILL EVER WASH OUT!!

Lava lover

More baking soda and vinegar madness, this volcano is good fun to make at home for no other reason than you can. It makes a great background for small plastic dinosaurs and it will also blow the teacher's mind if the kids ever have to do a geography project.

Mix together 600g plain flour, 400g salt, 4 tbsp of vegetable oil, 250ml water and a few drops of green and red food colouring. It should eventually become a smooth dough that's a murky, rocky brown sludge colour.

Get hold of another empty fizzy pop bottle (you can tell that these are going to be popular). The size of the bottle depends on how big you want your volcano to be. About 1 litre should be big enough for the dough recipe above. Fill it almost to the top with warm water and 6 drops of washing-up liquid, then add some red food colouring. Then you have to move briskly because you don't want the water going cold. Cover the bottle in the dough, in a mountain shape, going right up to the top but don't cover over the end of the bottle.

Add 2 tbsp of baking soda, then slowly pour the vinegar in the top. Krakatoa time!

Grape escape

Most people are well-versed in the dos and don'ts of microwave 'cookery', i.e. do pierce the film before putting the ready meal on high, don't put a ready meal in that's still in its metal container. And if you forget, the ensuing explosion/fireworks is enough to make sure you don't to it again. So let's do it on purpose shall we?

Take one grape (variety not thought to be important), and one microwave. Slice grape lengthways, leaving the two halves attached at one end by a small sliver of skin. Place face down on a microwaveable plate and put in microwave. Turn on to full power and turn on.

After about 5 seconds a fairly impressive light show should take place in the microwave, with sparks and flares coming from the grape. Eventually, the force of the fire will push the grapes apart and the light show will end. The result is a singed grape and a faint smell of burning grape juice. The microwave should escape unharmed.

K is for cooking

Unsurprisingly, the main function of the kitchen is to make food for the starving hordes. But there's nothing in the rulebook to say the starving hordes can't make the food themselves.

Obviously, if they haven't yet mastered standing up or spoon-feeding then it's probably best if Mum takes control of the bits involving scalding hot water and flames, but otherwise a bit of mixing, measuring and beating gives the result the all important 'I made it myself' tag. Another incentive for kids to cook is that it invariably involves sugar or chocolate.

Finally, if you can't face the misshapen, slightly burnt offerings there's bound to be some school fête around the corner demanding 'a small contribution' from each child. Be careful what you wish for, I say.

Fairy cakes

These are really easy for kids to make, and due to the simplicity of ingredients and the speed with which they're ready, excellent if you've got to get something cake-flavoured out at speed.

> 125g self-raising flour
> 125g caster sugar
> 125g margarine or softened butter
> 2 large eggs
> 4 drops vanilla essence OR zest of 1 lemon OR 2 tbsp cocoa powder
> 2 tbsp milk
> Squirty or whipped cream

Throw everything except the milk and cream into a bowl and beat to death, preferably with an electric whisk unless you want muscles like an East German shotputter. When it's all mixed in, put the first of the tablespoons of milk in, and beat again. If the mix still looks a bit dry, chuck in the other tablespoon of milk. The mix should look quite 'moussy' – I believe this is a technical cookery term … The longer you beat, the fluffier the mix, but a couple of minutes is more than enough.

Line a muffin tin with some cake cases and fill each with the mix. If you use cupcake cases the mix will pretty much fill them. The cupcakes should end up rising in quite high peaks above the edge of the case. Cook at 200°C for 20 minutes until golden brown.

If you have nice peaks, cut them off. It may seem brutal but you need them for your fairy 'wings'. Dollop some cream on top of the cakes, then cut the tops in half through the peak and stick into the cream at an angle.

Being able to turn out 12 fairy cakes in under 30 minutes is helpful when kids announce on their way to bed that: 'Oh, I need to take a cake to school for harvest festival/lunch.' It's also easy enough to hand the spatula and scales over and get them to do it themselves.

Chocolate crispies

While these are so simple to make even a dad could do it, there's that frustrating 12 hours where you have to hang about while they set. Faced with chocolatey goodies, dads and kids can't wait that long. It's best to put them somewhere out of sight.

Take 1 box of rice krispies and 1 big block of plain chocolate (you can use milk chocolate if you like but I find it makes them a bit sickly). Place a large bowl into a bain marie (a pan of simmering water). Break the chocolate into the bowl and melt slowly over a gentle heat. Stir now and again to make sure it melts evenly. Resist the temptation to lick the spoon.

Take the chocolate goo off the heat and start adding handfuls of krispies, stirring all the time. Stir gently because you don't want to reduce the krispies to powder. Keep adding krispies until all of the chocolate is used up and all the krispies are coated and sticky.

Spoon mixture into muffin cases and leave somewhere cool (and out of reach) to set.

Gingerbread men

These biscuits don't have to be man-shaped – you can use whatever cutters you have to hand. Invest in some festive ones to make cheap, tasty Christmas-tree decorations and save a small fortune in dangly chocolate Santas that taste suspiciously of dog drops.

300g plain flour
pinch salt
1 tsp baking powder
1 tsp allspice
ground black pepper(!)
100g margarine or softened butter
100g brown sugar

2 large eggs
4 tbsp honey

The easiest thing is to bung it all in a food processor, dry ingredients first, followed by wet. If you don't have one, you'll have to beat by hand. It should all come together in a pastry-like dough. Roll it out to the thickness desired of your biscuit and use shaped cutters to make the cookies. Cook on a baking sheet for 20 mins at 170°C. The pepper is what makes it gingery believe it or not!

If you want to decorate the men, make a simple glacé icing with icing sugar and water and dribble over once cooled. At the pre-cooking stage, poke small holes in the dough for gingerbread eyes, buttons and nose.

Chocolate truffles

25g cocoa powder
50g icing sugar
50g chopped hazelnuts
50g chopped glacé cherries
50g Philadelphia cream cheese
Desiccated coconut to roll them in

Put all the ingredients in a bowl and stir until it's all well mixed. Scoop a heaped teaspoon of the mixture into the palm of your hand and roll into a ball. It's better if your hands are cold because they can get pretty sticky.

Pour a good covering of desiccated coconut onto a large plate or small tray. Roll each truffle around in it until completely covered. Store in the fridge or cool cupboard until scoffing.

A tip for grown-ups: you can add a measure or two of rum, sherry or whisky to the mix for a headier bite. If this makes the mixture too sticky to roll, add another tablespoon of cocoa powder and icing sugar respectively.

Peppermint creams

500g icing sugar
4 tbsp condensed milk
oil of peppermint
green food colouring
small bar plain chocolate

Mix sugar, milk and a capful of colouring together until it makes a smooth, soft, minty-green dough. Start with three drops of peppermint and knead. Taste to see if minty enough. If not, add more mint a drop at a time.

Dust the surface with icing sugar and roll the dough into a long thin sausage. Break off a bit about the length of your thumb and roll into a ball. Then gently squash the middle with your thumb so it has a nice dent in it. Put in the fridge to harden.

Break the bar of chocolate into bits and melt in a bain marie (see page 80). Take the melted goo off the heat and dip some of the creams halfway in. Put on some greaseproof paper to set.

Hot tips for cooking sugar

- Follow measurements exactly.
- Don't boil the mixture until the sugar has completely dissolved.
- Stir with a wooden spoon, scraping the bottom and sides to prevent build-up.
- Keep a sugar thermometer in a mug of hot water before testing the mix, and put it back in there afterwards.
- Put the pan on a wet tea towel to stop the mix cooking more when you've taken it off the heat.

Butterscotch

150ml water

5ml lemon juice

500g granulated sugar

¼ tsp cream of tartar

90g unsalted butter

¼ tsp vanilla extract

Grease a 11 x 7in (28 x 18cm) baking tin. Heat the water and lemon juice gently, add the sugar and keep stirring until it has all dissolved. Don't let it boil.

If you don't have a sugar thermometer, keep a cup of cold water close by – you can check how set the sugar mixture is by dropping some into the cold water. Stir the cream of tartar into the warm mixture and bring to the boil. Once the mix reaches 115°C, or forms a soft ball when a teaspoonful is dropped into the water, remove from the heat and beat in the butter.

Return to the hob and heat to 138°C, or when the mixture becomes stringy in cold water. Take off the heat and add the vanilla. Pour into the tin and leave in a cool place until nearly set. Mark small rectangles with a knife and when fully set (leaving overnight is best) break into bits and eat. If there's any left, store in an airtight tub to stop it going soft.

Treacle toffee

110g unsalted butter

2 tbsp water

1 tbsp white vinegar

450g soft brown sugar

225g black treacle

It's a similar method to Butterscotch (see above), and you can tell it's reached the right temperature using the methods overleaf.

Heat butter, water and vinegar gently until the butter is melted. Add sugar and treacle and allow to dissolve. Bring to the boil at 138°C (stringy temperature), then take off the heat, letting the frothing mix calm down before you pour onto the oiled baking sheet. Mark the surface and break up once set. Make a dentist's appointment.

Old-fashioned peanut brittle

170g granulated sugar

170g golden syrup

60ml water

3 tbsp butter

340g chopped peanuts

2 tsp vanilla essence

1 tsp baking powder

Tests for sugar temperature

Thread

110–114°C

Will make a fine thread if pressed together then pulled apart

Soft ball

114–118°C

Will make a small ball that can be squashed flat

Hard ball

118–138°C

The ball cannot be squashed

Small crack

138–152°C

Will separate into threads that snap cleanly

Hard crack

152–163°C

Will separate into hard, brittle threads

Caramel

174°C

Turns a golden colour

Gently heat sugar, syrup, water and butter, stirring until the sugar has dissolved. Bring to the boil and keep it there for three minutes. When the mixture reaches the soft ball stage (see box, page 84), add the nuts and continue to heat until the hard crack stage (see box, page 84), stirring all the time.

Take the pan off the hob and stir in the vanilla and baking powder until you get a good head of foam, then pour onto a greased baking tray. Tease the mixture gently into a rectangle shape. When fully cool and set, break into bits. Order new dentures.

Crystal candy

There's some debate about whether this constitutes food, or is an experiment, but it squeaked into the food section by its munchability.

rough, colourfast string
pencil
a clean glass jar
1 cup water
3 cups granulated sugar
food colouring

Tie a piece of string to the pencil, balance the pencil over the jar and let the string dangle down inside. The string should reach almost to the bottom and should not touch the sides of the jar either.

Bring the water to the boil in a pan. Take off the heat and add the sugar a teaspoon at a time, stirring to make sure it's all dissolved before adding the next one. Keep going until no matter how much you stir, the sugar stays at the bottom of the pan. Add a couple of drops of food colouring. Pour the mixture into the jar, keeping the remaining sugar in the pan. Discard the sugar.

Put the jar somewhere safe and check on it daily. After day one, you should see coloured sugar crystals starting to form on the string. They should keep growing for a week or so, when they can be removed, and eaten!

Chapter Six

Some wild stuff

My mum always used to complain that a game of golf was a waste of a perfectly good walk. I tend to agree, but only because all those tedious clubs and woods and wedges (aren't they shoes?) take up space in a bag that would be put to much better use being filled with lots of delicious food.

Walking is allegedly fabulous for the health but, unless there's something to distract me along the way, I lose interest after a while. The promise of getting something for nothing is the carrot I need to keep going (I am Scottish after all). It's also a good way of keeping the kids' attention and getting them to provide a valuable service at the same time. Little fingers are so much better at getting in under some of the undergrowth, and a child's natural fascination for creepy crawlies means they don't get freaked out when a spider leaps out from behind a big juicy blackberry.

Foodie forays

There is all manner of tasty nosh lurking under trees and in bushes if you know where to look. Some of it you can munch as you go, while some needs a bit of work when you get home to make it more edible. As far as I know, they've yet to discover a sun-dried tomato tree or a Twix bush. but I do like a bit of fresh bramble jelly on my toast …

Rules of picking free food

The fruit you are picking also sustains the local wildlife. If you completely strip the bushes of all the ripe fruit in one small area, you could end up starving Thumper. Try to spread your harvesting around a bit.

Don't pick anything if you're not 100% sure what it is. These descriptions tell you what to do with the fruit but we don't describe them – on purpose. The best way is to get someone to show you exactly what they look like in the flesh. Search online for local woodland associations or funghi forays that organise guided walks. Certainly look online for colour pictures that show you what you're looking for. Don't just rely on descriptions no matter how comprehensive they seem, as it is easy to misinterpret.

Even if the juiciest, most succulent thornless bush is just over that hedge, don't go there. If it's someone's private land, those berries belong to them, and picking them without permission is theft.

One word of caution: don't pick food that is growing next to busy roads. Plants ingest the environment around them and that means all the pollution and fuel fumes go straight into the produce.

Don't forget to give everything you have picked a good wash before eating. Also, you'll need to sterilise the jars and lids you are using by popping them into a pan filled with boiling water and leaving for about 10 minutes.

Fruit

Bilberries

Bilberries are very like the blueberries that you can buy in tiny quantities from the supermarket if you take out a small mortgage. They can be a bit sharp if you eat them straight from the bush but make really nice jam, pudding and pie when you get home. You need about 3lb of fruit to make a decent quantity of jam.

There's often only a few ripe bilberries to a bush and they're quite low down so, if you think you're going to get a good enterprise going with your

under-age slave labour, you might have a workers' strike before long.

It is sometimes possible to find blueberry bushes here and there, and you can eat the fruit from the bush because, if it's ripe, it's nice and sweet. But, they really are few and far between in the wild.

Pick 'em: July–September.

Bilberry jam

Clean 3lb fruit and put in big pan with 1½lb sugar and 250ml water. (Apple juice instead of water makes the jam set harder as it contains pectin.) Boil for 40 mins. Strain the liquid through muslin (or an old tea towel, or a – clean! – pair of tights) to get out any bits of tree that are left. Pour into jars while still hot.

Elderflowers/berries

Elderflowers are famous for a ye olde type of cordial that's very subtle and quite grown-up. Unfortunately, despite the fact that the flowerheads of the plant are huge, blowsy things, you still need lots of them to make the squash. But, you can just snap off a flower or two and chomp on that instead.

The flowers turn to berries around August and last until October. You can tell that they're ready when they start to dangle upside down. Again, they're not a great instant eat, but good for pies or jam. Because the berries are so small and numerous, a good tip is to run a fork down the stems which knocks them all off in one go.

Pick 'em: June.

Elderberry pie

Get some of that frozen pre-roll pastry, defrost and use one of the circles to line a tin. Bake without any filling for 20 mins at 200°C. Layer with 600ml berries. Mix 100ml sugar, 2 tbsp of plain flour and a generous pinch of salt and scatter over the berries. Squeeze the juice of one lemon all over. Cover with the other circle of pastry. Prick to let steam out and bake for 10 mins at 200°C, then a further 30 mins at 170°C.

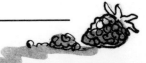

Crab apples

Like its namesake in *The Simpsons*, the crab apple is bitter and sharp when eaten raw, and can give you a bit of a stomach-ache. However, warm it up a bit and it can be very sweet, goes with anything and can even be intoxicating. Usually, the jelly goes on scones but it's equally good with roast meat in place of something like redcurrant or cranberry jelly.

Pick 'em: July–December.

Crab-apple jelly

This is one of the easiest free noshes to make. Wash the fruit, cover with water and boil for about 40 mins. Dig out your new tights and hang them over a big pan. Pour your boiled mush into the tights and leave to drip through overnight. If you try to force it all through the mesh you'll have a cloudy jelly that isn't as pretty. Boil up again using 1lb sugar to every pint of liquid. You don't need the extra special pectin sugar this time because there's loads of it in crab apples already.

A more grown-up alternative is to ferment the apples to make cider, although my student attempts at fruit and alcohol involved honey, water and an exploding Smirnoff bottle so I'm not to keen on going there again. You can, however, flavour booze with crab apples quite safely, making a concoction called 'Lamb's Wool'. Mix together some bitter, mushed-up roasted apples (pips etc. removed) and a sprinkling of sugar and spice (nutmeg, cinnamon and allspice are good). It was Shakespeare's tipple of choice.

Brambles

Brambles (also known as blackberries) are my all-time favourite food to pinch from the hedgerow. They're never confused with something poisonous, there are millions of them so you don't have to trawl far and wide, they grow up so you don't have to bend down and you can eat them on the spot, as well as using them in pies and jams. Hot brambles taste great with vanilla ice cream. My grandma always had a ready supply of them but she cheated by growing them up the back wall of her house.

Brambles are also the primary reason bird poo goes purple, which never fails to surprise me. Another thing that shocks my socks off about brambles is that supermarkets sell them at the same scary prices as blueberries. And you only get about 12 in a punnet. They probably grow in their hundreds round the corner from your house, which is nearer than the supermarket and you're still *paying for them?* And before you complain that you live in central Birmingham, they grow just as well in inner-city parks as they do in darkest Norfolk.

Pick 'em: August–29 September.

Brapple Crumple

Take 100g cold butter, chopped into cubes. Rub in 100g plain flour with your fingers until it resembles fine breadcrumbs. Stir in 100g porridge oats and 100g brown sugar. Core and thinly slice four good, rustic-type apples (if it's windfall season, pinch them from the ground under neighbouring apple trees to keep the whole freegan ethic – check for worms!). Toss with 150g brambles and 3 tbsp sugar. Grease a pie dish and lay fruit on the bottom. Sprinkle crumple mixture evenly over the top and put in the oven at 190°C for 40 mins until the crumple is crispy. Spoon over ice cream. Enjoy.

Damsons

Damsons have history. Lots of it. They were one of the Romans' favourite fruits and historians reckon that it was the Crusaders who brought them back to England. Not unlike small plums, they're still quite bitter even when ripe so they're best eaten cooked, and are again hot candidates for the jam/jelly department. With a healthy dollop of cream, sugar and pastry, however, they make a fine cobbler.

Pick 'em: August–September.

Damson cobbler

Cover 1kg damsons with water and 225g sugar and stew to a pulp, remove stones and put in a greased pie dish. Mix 225g self-raising flour, 1 tsp

baking powder and 25g sugar and rub in 55g margarine. Add 7 tbsp milk and pound into a dough. Cut into circles (if you haven't got cookie cutters, use a small cup). Layer the rounds on top of the mixture so they overlap slightly, brush with a little more milk and cook for 30 mins at 190°C.

Rosehips

Rosehips saved Britain during the Second World War. Without them, our parents and grandparents would have gone ga-ga through scurvy and their legs would have dropped off. Maybe. German U-boats blockaded supplies of vitamin-C bearing oranges and lemons so it had to be found from elsewhere. The average homemade rosehip syrup contains 65mg of vitamin C per fluid ounce. Even better, rosehips grew like a weed and were free.

Schoolkids were encouraged to 'do their bit' and in 1941 they were among the volunteers sent out to collect rosehips. In 1942, around 344 tons were gathered for the nation. Collecting continued even after the war, as kids were paid a token amount for each pound they collected. A secondary school in Carlisle got a really good cottage industry going, and amassed more than 30,000lb in 1964. Unfortunately for today's kids, the payment incentive is no longer there, but the syrup can still be made quite easily. And it'll knock the history teacher's socks off if they need a project on the war. **Pick 'em:** September–November.

1941 Ministry of Food rosehip syrup recipe

Boil 3pt (1.7l) boiling water. Mince 2lb (900g) hips and put immediately into the boiling water. Bring to a boil and then place aside for 15 minutes. Pour into a flannel or linen crash jelly bag [out come the tights again] and allow to drip until the bulk of the liquid has come through.

Return the residue to the saucepan, add 1½pt (852ml) of boiling water, stir and allow to stand for 10 minutes. Pour back into the jelly bag and allow to drip. To make sure all the sharp hairs (if swallowed these really irritate the lining of the stomach) are removed, put back the first half cupful of liquid and allow to drip through again.

Put the mixed juice into a clean saucepan and boil down until the juice measures about 1½pt (852ml), then add 1¼lbs (560g) of sugar and boil for a further 5 minutes. Pour into hot sterile bottles and seal at once. It is advisable to use small bottles as the syrup will not keep for more than a week or two once the bottle is opened. Store in a dark cupboard.

If you can't wean the ankle biters off Ribena, then you can also make ice-lollies from the syrup. You may not want to tell them that the ground-down seeds of the rosehip make an excellent itching powder ...

Sloes

Sloes are quite hard to get at and it's handy to have some small fingers willing to do the work for you. They are the fruit of the blackthorn tree, which has some fairly vicious thorns. There is a story that the thornbird is a beautiful sounding thrush-like bird that sings its sweetest song just before it flies into a thorn bush, impaling itself on the thorns and dying.

Sloes do make reasonable jam but they're put to even better use in gin. Sloe gin is a really warming liqueur excellent for a hipflask on a cold walk. Not for the kids though. They'll have to make do with rosehip syrup.

Pick 'em: October–November.

Sloe gin, fast drink

If you pick the sloes before the first frost, you'll need to prick the skins to help the fruit juice mix with the gin. Frost softens the skin for you. Mix the berries with the same weight of sugar and use to half fill a bottle. Pour the gin on top and seal tightly. Store somewhere dark and dry for at least two months, shaking occasionally to mix and dissolve the sugar. The gin will turn a dark pink and have quite a kick, and because they've been pickled in the sugar and gin for so long, the berries will be edible too. If you fancy, make a grown-up pud by straining out some of the alcoholic berries and sprinkling them on some cream or ice cream.

Nuts

Acorns

The fruit of the oak tree, acorns were commonly used during the Second World War as a replacement for real coffee, called ersatz meaning 'pretend'. It proves how desperate people can get for their caffeine hit because acorns aren't really the best replacement. They're pretty bitter and need a lot of soaking and roasting to get the sour taste out of them. You can, however, use them as a musical instrument instead.

Pick 'em: October.

Acorn whistling

Break the 'cup' of the bottom of the acorn. Hold it with both hands, pinching it between thumbs and the sides of your index fingers. Your thumbs should be resting back-to-back, with the tips facing away. This makes a Y-shape, leaving only a small slice of the acorn showing at the top.

Rest your thumb knuckles against your bottom lip, and as Lauren Bacall so famously said, just put your lips together and blow. By blowing the air round the cup of the acorn and over the top, you should get a neat whistling sound.

Hazelnuts

Also known as cobnuts, these grow well in woods all over the UK. However, they're a firm favourite of squirrels and seeing as the grey squirrel is becoming as ubiquitous as pigeons, hazelnuts are pretty hard to find.

Hazelnuts can be used in salads and main dishes or as snacks. Alternatively, roast them and pour melted chocolate over the top. Let it harden and you've made your own fruit and nut. Ok, so you'll have to throw in a few raisins as well to make the fruit bit.

Pick 'em: August–October.

Chestnuts

These are another nut that you have to fight the squirrel for. But beware beware beware. There are two types of chestnut: the horse chestnut is commonly called a conker and used for marmalising small boys' knuckles. It is also poisonous. The sweet chestnut is for roasting on an open fire, Jack Frost nipping at your nose ...

The problem is that while on the tree they look different enough to make the distinction easily, once they've hit the floor and split open, the kernel inside both looks almost identical. For that reason, only pick sweet chestnuts for eating that fall off the tree in front of your eyes (with or without the help of a big stick), or are still mostly inside their shells on the ground.

Sweet chestnuts can be just shelled and roasted, or roasted and mashed and mixed with sugar to make a sweet purée to put inside biscuits. You can even make ice cream from them. To add a bit of seasonal drama to the process, try the 'explosion' cooking technique. If you're lucky enough to have an open fire at home, slit the skins of all the shelled chestnuts *but one*, and put them in the hot ash or near the red coals. Then put in the one that hasn't had its skin slit. You might want to make sure you've got a fireguard in place. When the unslit one explodes, the others are ready to eat. The explosion can be pretty powerful, catapulting bits of red-hot chestnut and possibly bits of coal and log all over the place. You do *not* want to try this in a domestic oven unless you're Michael Caine and want to blow the bloody doors off. If you're a bit heartless, try it on a barbecue outside instead.

Pick 'em: late October–November.

Vegetables

Wild garlic

This is also called ramsons and it is kind of hard to miss. If you go into a nice dank, dark woodland where ramsons are growing, the whole place will hum to high heaven of garlic. And you'll wonder why you can't tell where the smell is coming from.

That's because it looks nothing like the bulb bit you're used to seeing. Instead, it's a bunch of wide, shiny green leaves, sometimes with a couple of tall thin stems with a cluster of white flowers at the top depending on the season.

Despite the really strong smell, the garlic taste is actually pretty mild if you cook the leaves. Instead, try mashing the leaves with parmesan and pine nuts (or hazelnuts if you can wrestle a couple off Squirrel Nutkin) to make a garlicky pesto. You can even eat the flowers, which taste a bit stronger than the leaves, again raw or cooked depending on the strength of vampire you need to get rid of.

Mushrooms

Picking wild mushrooms is like the bungee jumping of the food world. It's extreme eating! That's because for every tasty, risotto-bound fungus, there's another that will kill you before you can say *Amanita virosa*.

People are quite rightly nervous, even fearful, of collecting mushrooms from the wild. I'm quite happy for things to stay that way. But it doesn't mean that you can't go and get some *boletus edulis* to go with your ramson and cobnut risotto and brapple crumple for pud. You just need to know exactly what you're doing.

The best way to learn is to go on a fungi foray – organised walks with experts who can point out what you can and can't pick and how to recognise them. You can look the varieties up on the web and print off some good pictures of what they look like but there's nothing like first-hand expert advice to make you feel safe.

Here are a few of the most common 'shrooms kicking around the UK's woods:

Cepes (*Boletus edulis*): The mere mention of these makes chefs go all runny at the mouth. Otherwise known as porcini, you can buy them dried at the supermarket but they cost a mint. Unfortunately, flies seem to think they make good childcare centres, which means they can be full of maggots – give them a thorough check over before tucking in.

Parasol (*Lepiota procera*): The good news is that it's really hard to mistake a poisonous mushroom for this one so if it looks like a parasol, it is a parasol. The bad news is that they're very difficult to find, not because they're in hiding, but because they're rare. Parasols have a very delicate taste. If you find a few, invite the neighbours over for dinner so you can show off.

Hedgehog fungus (*Hydnum repandum*): Like its namesake, this one likes to hide in the undergrowth, but once you've got used to looking for it, it's quite easy to find. It's also hard to mistake it for a poisonous one so you can feel quite secure that you're not going to turn yourself into mushroom compost by eating it.

Deceiver (*Laccaria laccata*): These ones are quite easy to find so once you've got the hang of them and you know where they grow, it can be a rewarding trip to go and get some knowing that you'll come back with more than a twig and a runny nose. They're a bit chameleon-like, though, changing shape as they mature. One for seasoned 'shroomers.

Cauliflower fungus (*Sparassis crispa*): A fantastic mushroom for teenage boys to present before dinner and claim that it's 'brains for tea again, Mother!'. This fungi is a parasite that lives off tree roots so you'll find it at the bottom of trees. It looks gruesomely brain-shaped, complete with

wiggly vessels and everything. But if you can get over the cerebellum/tripe resemblance, it's supposed to be pretty tasty (I can't get over the 'brain' bit yet).

Don't even ... Not ever

The following are just two of the fairly rare, poisonous fungi lurking in the woods. Don't touch.

Destroying Angel (*Amanita virosa*): This looks very elegant and fragile in a Miss Haversham kind of way with its pure white top. They're not big and half of one single fungus is enough to kill an average-size adult.

Fly agaric (*Amanita muscaria*): This grows all over the place but thanks to the fact that it's pretty distinctive it shouldn't give you any problems. You'd have to eat a fairly large quantity to actually kill yourself, but just one can induce some fairly freaky hallucinations.

Plant games

There are of course things you can do with plants that don't involve eating them (I *know*! What a *waste*!).

Buttercups

The story goes that if you hold a buttercup under your chin and it reflects yellow, you will either be very rich, or you like butter. I know which version I prefer. If it doesn't shine yellow then the reverse is true.

Lucky leaf

Clover is a maddening thing. You spend ages trying to get the stuff out of your lawn and then tell the kids that four-leaf clovers bring luck, and the kids start moaning that you don't have any 'lucky grass' in the back garden. Most clover is of the three-leafed variety and is also known as the Shamrock, Ireland's national emblem.

Perhaps the idea that a four-leaf clover is lucky stems from the fact that they are pretty rare, or could it come from the idea that it too is a Shamrock and therefore benefits from 'the luck of the Irish'? There seems no concrete reason why it is lucky, just that it was considered lucky as far back as the Druids so who am I to argue? Here's a little clover ditty for you:

I'm looking over a four-leaf clover
That I overlooked before.
One leaf is sunshine, the second is rain,
Third is the roses that grow in the lane.
No need explaining the one remaining
Is somebody I adore.
I'm looking over a four-leaf clover
That I overlooked before.

Pooh sticks

So-called because Winnie-the-Pooh often took time out of his packed Hunny-finding schedule to race twigs down a river under a bridge with his best friend Piglet (or should that be Twiglet?). Seems a bit simple but it can get surprisingly competitive.

A bridge is the traditional racecourse observation point, but provided all contestants agree on a clearly defined start and finish line, any stretch of river will do nicely. Start by facing the upstream side of the river. Choose your 'Pooh stick'. It can be a twig, a flower or anything that's easily identifiable as yours. You don't all want to have matching sticks or there'll be a fight over who won. Nor do you want them to be too different or someone will claim the others had an unfair advantage because their stick was fatter/thinner/wider/shorter. A tip: stones don't work.

Count down three … two … one and simultaneously throw your sticks as far upstream off the bridge as you can. Then race over to the other side of the bridge and wait for your stick to emerge victorious.

Loves me, loves me not

If you want to keep a lovesick teenager occupied for a few minutes, give them a flower with lots of petals. Daisies are good, dandelions are better. Tell them they can predict their romantic future by plucking off each petal reciting loves me for the first petal, loves me not for the next, and so on. If the outcome should unfortunately be loves me not, insist that it was obviously a lop-sided flower and they should try another one for a more 'reliable' answer.

Chapter Seven

Some magic stuff

I f you really want to demonstrate the power and genius of the mum, you need nothing more than a bit of magic accompanied by a spot of speaking in tongues. This is the sort of behaviour that would have probably got you burned at the stake in the ever-so-slightly paranoid mid-1600s.

Today, though, you'll probably just attract the odd sideways glance. You don't need any special equipment, other than a cup of tea, a pack of cards and a knowing smile. You'll also be able to hold a huge amount of power over your kids, who won't quite be able to tell if you're mucking about or not.

Reading tea-leaves

Grandmas used to think they were great at doing this sort of thing, but I think it was to cover the fact that they hadn't used a strainer when pouring out the tea. If you find bits of garden lurking at the bottom of your cup, leave the last sip and read your fortune with it instead.

1   Always use a bone china teacup and saucer, not a mug. No proper reason, but youngsters just don't understand the etiquette of afternoon tea any more.

2   Leave a mouthful of tea with the leaves in the bottom.

3   Swirl the remaining liquid around the cup, clockwise, three times and then turn the cup upside down on the saucer, letting the last liquid run out.

4   Turn the cup the right way up again and hold with the handle of the cup facing you.

5   Now all you need to do is look for discernible shapes that can predict the future. This may take a bit of practise and no small amount of bluffing. It's a bit like lying outside in the dark with some smartipants pointing out Cassiopea in the stars. All you can see is a bit of tree, the end of the big bear (everyone can see that one) and the 9:30 departure from Heathrow to JFK.

AIRCRAFT – journey

AXE – difficulties

BELL – unexpected news

BIRDS – good news

BUSH – new friend

CANDLE – help from others

CHAIN – engagement or wedding

CIRCLE – success, with dots means a baby

COIN – money

CROSS – suffering

CUP – reward

EGG – good omen

FISH – good fortune

FLAG – danger

FORKED LINE – decision

GUN – anger

HAMMER – hard work needed

HEART – love

HORSESHOE – good luck

HOUSE – security

JEWELS – gifts

MOUSE – theft

QUESTION MARK – caution

RING – marriage

ROSE – popularity

SCISSORS – fights

SPIDER – reward for work

STAR – health and happiness

SUN – success

TREE – improvements

VOLCANO – harmful emotions

WHEEL – good fortune

WINGS – messages

Reading fruit

One of the most common ways of telling fortunes used to be to peel an apple and throw the skin over your left shoulder. The peel had to come off the apple entirely in one whole strip or it was bad luck. The shape of the letter it made when it fell on the floor was the initial of your husband-to-be. The best time to do this would be Halloween, and it's even got a witchy-type rhyme of its very own:

> *If your future hubby's name you wish to know*
> *Over your left shoulder an apple peel throw*
> *It will wriggle and coil, and you will see*
> *The first initial of who it will be*
> *For the witches plot and the hexes scheme*
> *On the mystic night of Halloween.*

Once you've got rid of the apple peel, it's time to look inside for a bit more futurology:

Reading apple pips

Take a whole apple, cut it and count the pips.

Use this list to tell your fortune:

1 = A surprise in the near future

2 = Good luck

3 = Bad luck

4 = Wealth

5 = An early marriage

6 = Fame

7 = Travel

Reading palms

Palmistry is another common way of freaking the kids out. There are three main creases in each hand and their characteristics are a way of predicting someone's future. Contrary to popular belief, a short so-called 'life line' does not contribute to a short life overall.

To tell a future based on reading palms, you first need to break down what each bit means. First, no two hands are the same. The right hand is considered to be your practical side. It is the one responsible for getting things done. This applies even if you are left-handed. Your left hand relates to your emotional side, and deals with affairs of the heart.

On each hand, you have three main lines: the heart line, the head line and the life line. The heart line is closest to your fingers, followed by the head line in the middle and then the life line, which most commonly curves around the thumb and travels vertically down the centre of the palm.

If the shape of your heart line:
- Becomes a steep curve below the index and the middle finger – you really fancy someone

- Stops under your index finger – you're a bit choosy
- Stops under your middle finger – you're a bit needy
- Is straight and short – you're not very romantic
- There are two or more strokes, or branches coming out of the line – that's how many different sides there are to you emotionally
- There's a branch that comes down and meets the life line – you're easily hurt
- If it matches your partner's – you'll be happy together

If the shape of your head line:

- Stops under your ring finger (of either hand) – you're pretty average
- Is short – a simple thinker
- Is long – a profound thinker
- Is straight – a clear thinker
- Is curved – open-minded
- Slopes – creative
- Horizontal – practical
- Is broken into a series of links – highly strung
- Is forked – open-minded (again)
- Starts under your index finger – brilliant

If the shape of your life line:

- Is close to your thumb – a bit tired
- Has a wide curve – lot of energy
- Deeper than the head line – more into sport than intellectual pursuits
- Is broken in links – sickly
- Has fine lines that rise from the curve – bouncy
- Has lines that curve away from the curve – adventurer
- Has lines crossing through the life line – indicates life events

Tarot cards

Cartomancers – isn't that a great name? – is the term for people who read fortunes on decks of cards. 'My mum's a cartomancer,' has a certain ring to it. Of course, Tarot cards are famous for the one Death card that is usually suitably gory, featuring a skeleton or the grim reaper. The Hanging Man is another popular one for freaking people out. In fact, neither of them is that literal. Death usually means change or a warning not to get too big for your boots and the Hanging Man means that you should take some time out to think about things.

But you don't need fancy Tarot cards to do a reading. Your average 52-strong pack of cards will do a nice job of telling fortunes, provided you know what each of them means:

How to do a Tarot reading

Wrap the cards in a silky piece of cloth to add to the whole mysticism of the reading event. Unwrap them in front of the subject and find out what question they want to ask: Will I get good exam results? Will Gary from 4B dump Claire and go out with me? Concentrate on the question and shuffle the deck well. Hand the cards to the questioner and ask them to cut the pack, while asking the question out loud.

Deal the top four cards in a diamond shape. The card at the top point represents romance, the next on the right is finance, the third at the bottom is health and happiness and the fourth on the left is career. Use the basic meanings and embellish, ahem, I mean interpret accordingly.

General	Hearts	Clubs	Diamonds	Spades
	emotions, pain	relationships	problems (especially money)	warnings
Ace	home	wealth	important mail	bad news
King	a powerful man	a good friend	bitter rival	causes problems in marriages
Queen	a trusted woman	wife or sister	flirty, interfering woman	cruel
Jack	a good friend	flatterer and friend	selfish, bearer of bad news	layabout
10	good luck	happiness	greed	unlucky
9	harmony or a wish	arguments	adventure	misery
8	a party	desperation (especially money)	travel or late marriage	betrayal
7	disappointment	good luck	bad luck	sorrow
6	being used	partnership	short-lived marriage	discouragement
5	indecisive	marriage	prosperity, fecundity	success after hard work
4	unmarried/picky	danger	quarrels	temporary setback
3	bad decisions	successive marriages	disputes	unhappiness
2	success	bad luck	love affair	big, bad change

Atwhay oday ouyay aysay?

(What do you say?)

You spend most of your kids' infant years trying to figure out what they're saying, experience a brief period of clarity where you both seem to be communicating before the teenage years begin and then everything gets lost in translation again. It's bad enough when they just mumble normal English, but if they get the hang of a secret language (other than CU2NITE, DONTBL8) then you're really in trouble.

Secret languages are nothing new. Families used to invent whole languages for their own amusement. Several aristocratic families thought it awfully funny to talk only in their own language when they had visitors. Costermongers in the East End of London began Cockney Rhyming Slang as a secret language. The word 'slang' comes from 'secret **lang**uage'.

There are all sorts of different names for these languages, but the common term for them is Pig Latin.

There are pros and cons to teaching kids secret languages. On the one hand, you can all enjoy a good giggle when you gossip about someone in front of them. On the downside, it doesn't take much to alter the rules so you can't understand it, and they start saying all sorts of things about you instead.

For words that begin with a single consonant, take the consonant off the front of the word and add it to the end of the word. Then add 'ay' after the consonant:

cat = atcay
dog = ogday
simply = implysay
noise = oisnay

For words that began with double or multiple consonants, take the group of consonants off the front of the word and add them to the end, adding 'ay' at the very end of the word:

scratch = atchscray
thick = ickthay
flight = ightflay
grime = imegray

For words that begin with a vowel, just add 'yay' at the end. For example:

is = isyay
apple =appleyay
under = underyay
octopus = octopusyay

Chapter Eight

Some fancy stuff

here's nothing better than getting dressed up for an evening out. Getting the outfit together. Choosing accessories. Putting on the lipstick, eyeliner, beheading scar and eye patch. It's all very well putting on a new party frock but it's nowhere near as much fun as getting dressed up as the bog mummy and heading off to terrorise small children.

Of course, the idea is that these costumes are made for small children but there's nothing to stop you organising an impromptu 'vicars and tarts' do to put your new-found skills to the test.

Most of these outfits are designed for one-off use and are perfectly good enough for a quick party, school play or some 'trick or treating' at Halloween.

If you are getting ready for a competition, however, you might want to use some better materials. The theory is the same but, instead of glueing, you might want to sew, and in the place of decorating with paper, you could use cloth or felt, which glues well onto other cloth. Either way, they're all eminently adaptable.

In all cases, you should rope in as many helpers as possible to glue, stuff, fluff, doodle, design, chop and staple. Chanel got paid for doing this sort of thing you know …

The bog mummy

The ultimate in quick-fix fancy dress that you can literally throw together on your way out of the door.

Get your mummy-to-be to stand legs slightly apart and arms bent at the elbow, wrists limp. Start at one ankle with a roll of toilet paper and just start winding. To prevent premature unravelling, make the first few winds in the same place before you start climbing up the leg. Stop when you get to the top of the thigh and tuck the end in. Repeat with the other leg.

For authenticity, you can make a kind of nappy around the bum, but some may not appreciate that much attention to detail. Wind in circles around the torso, working your way from the lower waist up to the armpits, then continuing criss-cross from under one armpit to over the opposite shoulder until you reckon you've got enough coverage. Do the arms like the legs, remembering to keep the arms bent while you're winding to maintain that authentic, zombie look.

If you want to go the whole hog, wind more loo roll round the head and under the chin and top it all off with some white face paint and some good dark circles around the eyes.

Don't try to be too neat. Before you wind each new limb, start a few sheets in so you've got some trailing 'bandages'.

Three important points

1   Going for the full nappy option is only a short-term option. Trying to figure out where the stray end is when you're busting for the loo is a bit of a delicious irony. And you'd be surprised how hard it is to rip through several layers of tightly wound toilet paper.

2   Don't use every single roll of paper in the house after the shops have shut. That's a surefire way to guarantee someone gets Delhi belly the moment 'mummy' leaves the premises.

3   It's got to be white, white, white all the way. Peach dream is wrong on so many levels.

The bin-bag costumes

If you're pushed for time and resources, there is always going to be something you can make, provided you've got a stash of handy bin bags and a stapler.

Witch costume

Being a witch is rubbish. Literally. Apart from the hat, for which a big bit of black cardboard would be handy, you can find everything you need next to the bin.

Take a roll of black bin bags and tear off 10 or so. 'Fluff' each of them out. Take one bag, and cut a hole in the bottom big enough to get your head through. Then cut two holes at the sides a couple of inches up from the bottom for the arms. This makes the basic tunic.

Take the waistband or a leg from an old pair of black tights, anything that will go all the way around your waist comfortably and you can staple things to.

Take another bin bag and cut along the bottom seam and up one side to make a cape. If yours is one of those posh bin bags with a built-in tie, you can either cut the black plastic gently away from it leaving it intact as an automatic tie to keep the cape on. Or, if junior is at risk of choking, cut it out and staple the cape to the shoulders of the tunic instead.

For the witchy skirt, take the rest of the puffed-out bags and scrunch the open ends together. Tie the ends tight with an elastic band, string or sellotape, and staple through it to your waistband. Work all the way round so that the bags are evenly spaced but don't have too many gaps when you're standing still.

Take your big bit of black cardboard and roll into a cone. Fix with staples, glue or sellotape and cut along the bottom (that's the wide end for those who have worn this shape of hat before) so it's even. Paint face green, steal a black cat and go round turning princes into frogs.

Fairy costume

Skirt: Using the same principle as the witch costume above, make a sturdy belt from card. To the belt, staple glittery, fairy-like materials such as white plastic shopping bags (no tell-tale Tesco logos, please); clear plastic shopping bags; fancy coloured shopping bags in hot pink, bright yellow or silver. You can go bohemian and have a bit of everything in there, or for your loft-living, minimalist fairy, stick to one colour throughout. As with the witch costume, the closer together you staple the bags, the fuller the effect.

Wings: Take two all-metal coathangers. There should be plenty in the wardrobe as most kids I know hang their clothes on the floor these days. With the help of a bit of brute force, pull the coathangers apart until, sideways on, they make a diamond shape. Then squash the first hook down until it meets the spiral part and forms an enclosed circle.

Decorate with whatever sparkly nonsense you have to hand. You can fill the centre of each wing with chiffon, muslin, old net curtain, *new* net curtain and even tracing paper. Cut out a shape that's about half a centimetre bigger than the coathanger all round (it doesn't need to be exact), then fold it around the frame and glue. If you want to be really fancy, you can sew it round the edges with thin satin ribbon.

If you leave the centres empty, let the frame make a statement. Wrap it in the fluffiest tinsel you can find, dangle Christmas baubles from the top part, or even brightly wrapped sweeties. Unlike the tooth fairy, I always preferred the sweet fairy; however, as with many of life's ironies, I came to discover that the two were inextricably linked.

To tie on: First, hook the second as yet unbent coathanger loop through the first, then bend it shut. Thread a good, wide bit of satin ribbon about 2m long through the first loop and back out through the second. Pull the ribbon until the ends are roughly even. Loop over the shoulders and pass under the armpits. Tuck each end through a loop and tie in a bow at the back.

Batwings

We're back to the black bin bags again. Take two bin bags and cut along the base and up one side of both. Open out flat. Cut a convex arc (i.e. one that means there's more rather than less of the bag left once you've finished) from the top left to bottom right corner. Fold the bag in half from the top left to bottom right corner, once, and then once again, so it looks like a flattened cone. Now cut a deep concave arc (i.e. going the opposite way) across the bottom. Opening it out should give you the pointy batwing effect along the bottom.

Fix one of the straight edges of the batwing to the underside of the wearer's outfit, and the other to their side, making sure the pointy end is fixed just under the armpit. Use staples, quite close together, because despite puncturing the cloth, they won't really damage anything you want to wear again. Alternatively, use some black gaffer tape, which is quite strong but matches the wings and won't damage anything. Ordinary sellotape or glue just won't last the distance.

Christmas tree

Get hold of a roll of those green garden refuse sacks. You'll need about four or five bags. Cut along the bottom but not up the side. Do, however, cut the tie as it's easier to tie like a belt when there are two ends instead of a hoop.

Get the wearer to step into the first bag and tie it around the waist. Then pull the second bag over their head, get their arms through and tie it under the armpits. Get a third and pull it over the head and tie it round the neck (not too tight ...).

Trim the length of the bags until you have three layers at even distances from each other, without whatever your tree is wearing underneath showing through. Make the edges quite zig zaggy to look tree like. If it is bulky enough then leave it as it is, but if you feel that your tree looks a bit like a beanpole, add another bag round the waist and under the armpits, making sure that each layer is shorter than the one below it.

Top the tree by making a typical cone hat from stiff green paper. Try perching an angel or a star on the top for extra authenticity.

All you have to do now is decorate your tree. Try stapling some tinsel round the edges, and adding a few glitter stars and baubles. You might want to make the tree very popular by stapling lots of chocolate Santas to it. You may also give your child their very first experience of being mugged.

Basic tunic

If you're going to go to the trouble of making something out of cloth, it helps to have a one-size-fits-all pattern. Here are two for a tunic and a cape that cover most of the history and horror themes between them.

Measure the length of the body the tunic needs to cover. For recyclability, go for longer rather than shorter because you can always take it up and let it down again if you need to.

Get a piece of cloth twice that length and fold it double. Measure a space wide enough to get a head through comfortably and mark it in the middle of the fold at the top of the tunic. Draw a rectangle 4in deep by the width you measured across. Cut out to make a neck hole.

Leaving space for the arms and sleeves. Measure 12in down one side from the fold, then begin sewing all the way down to the bottom. Repeat for the other side. This is your basic tunic shape.

With no sleeves, it's a good base for a gladiator outfit, a slave outfit or a Roman emperor outfit.

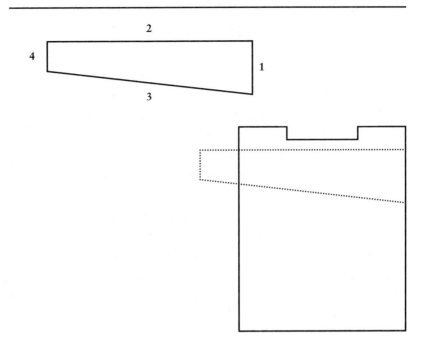

But if you're feeling really flash, you might want to add sleeves. Are you sure? They're a bit tricky ... well, a bit trickier than sewing the sides of a rectangle together, but not much.

It's helpful if you can map your measurements out on a bit of paper before transferring it to cloth. It's often hard to find ordinary paper that's long or wide enough for a full pattern, so use a roll of cheap wrapping paper. Just draw your pattern on the wrong side, or your measurements will be lost in a hail of gift-bearing penguins.

For the sleeve, measure the length of the gap you left in the tunic, and add 2cm to allow for the seam (1). Then measure the length of your arm from the edge of the shoulder (i.e. where the tunic ends) and your wrist. Add 2cm (2). This is the longest part of the sleeve and when you come to cut it out of cloth it is the bit that will be placed along the fold in the cloth.

Then measure the length from under the arm to the wrist (3). This measurement will undoubtedly be shorter than the one from the shoulder and forms the underside of the sleeve. Finally, measure round the clenched fist (4) – not the wrist! You want to make sure the sleeve will go over the hand. Unless you're using very stretchy material, if you make the end of your sleeve only wide enough for the wrist, the wearer will never be able to get their hand through it.

Divide the fist measurement in half and that's how long the sleeve end is from the fold.

Place the straight edge (2) along the fold in the cloth and cut out. Repeat for the other sleeve. Sew along the bottom between (1) and (4). Turn the right way out.

To attach the sleeve to the tunic, turn the tunic inside out and slot the sleeve into the hole from inside. Sew around edges, starting and ending with a double stitch so the arms don't spontaneously fall off.

Now you've got a basic tunic (do you see how much easier it is to make everything out of bin bags?). It will suit almost any outfit: a monk, a devil, a king, a knight, a wise man, a nun … the possibilities are endless. All you need to do is accessorise.

Basic cape

A good cape is simple to make and can really help to finish off an outfit. It turns a plain white shirt and black trousers into a vampire or a magician. Turn it inside out and you've got an instant devil.

While I'm a firm believer in using whatever you can get your hands on, in this case it's worth a trip to the shops. Satin is the cloth of choice for your discerning vampire, but lining material is a lot cheaper and just as shiny.

Take 1.5m red material, and a 1.5m of black material. Pin them together with the shiniest sides facing each other (i.e. on the inside). Sew all the way round leaving a gap of a couple of inches at the bottom so you can turn the cape right side out again; thus, hiding the seams. Stich the gap up as carefully and invisibly as you can.

Next, you need to make a channel about 3in from the top for the ribbon tie. This means sewing one row right across the cape, followed by another row about an inch below it. Now take a nice thick, shiny cloth ribbon in red, black or white about 2m long and put a safety pin through one end. You use this to 'feed' the ribbon through the channel.

Then all you need to do is throw the cape round your shoulders with a flourish, tie the ribbon and practise your best 'Mwah, hah-hah-haaaa!'.

Devil costume

If you've got a basic cape with red lining as described above then you're halfway there. It's best if you put it over a red T-shirt and trousers, not that many people have red trousers. Making trousers is even more of a faff than making sleeves and I wouldn't advise it, especially at short notice.

My basic standby when there aren't the right coloured trousers kicking about, is to get a pair of really thick woolly tights in the right colour – for both boys and girls. As long as the top is long enough to cover their modesty, it works.

So, armed with a red T-shirt, slinky cape and a fetching pair of tights, you only need a couple more items to complete the look – the tail and the horns. For the horns, track down a spare bit of red or black material. For the tail, a couple of metres of really wide slinky ribbon is good, plus some more of the horn material for the tail.

For the horns, you need to cut four triangles about 4in wide by 6in tall. Sew one triangle to another, making two pointy cups. If you sew one of the seams on each slightly concave then you'll have a nice 'horny' shape. Stuff them with some more of our trusty cut-up tights, or cotton wool, or tissues. Then grab the waistband from a pair of tights (closely matching the hair colour is best but it doesn't really matter) and sew the open triangles onto the tights so that the horns stick up. If you did the 'horny' shape, make sure the rounded edges are facing one another in a mirror image or it'll look weird. And not in a good way.

For the tail, sew the long edges of the ribbon all the way from one end to the other, with the shiny side facing inwards. Turn it right side out so you have a shiny tube and stuff with lots and lots of chopped-up tights until it's quite rigid. Sew the top end shut as invisibly as possible. Using some more of the horn material, draw two heart shapes, about 3in across at their widest point. Sew them together, leaving a gap between the 'bumps' of the heart big enough to turn the heart the right way out. Stuff with – yep – more tights/tissues/etc. Put the open end of the shiny tube into the heart and carefully sew the rest of the way around the heart shape, trying to keep the stitches as neat and as invisible as possible.

Pin the tail to the back of the tights with a sturdy safety pin and spray all over with eau de Brimstone for that sophisticated, devil-may-care look.

Ready chaps!

The iconic bit of the cowboy outfit, the chaps, work best if you use a grotty old pair of brown trousers. Traditionally, chaps are beaten-up old leather, there to protect cowboys' legs from whips, dips and muck. Corduroy is good as it's quite heavy and looks scruffy. Obviously, not everyone has these just kicking around but try raiding the local charity shops – I think they breed brown corduroy trousers. Don't worry if they don't fit – the bigger the better because they have to go on over your jeans, and flap about a bit into the bargain.

To make the shape of the chaps, you simply cut the bum out of them, front and back and all the way through. Look for a pair that has beltloops, then you can afford to cut all the way through the waistband. If not and they fit round the waist, leave the waistband on because you'll need something to hold them up.

Then cut from behind the knee down to the bottom of the trousers, taking out a V-shape the width of the back of the calf. Round off the bottoms so they flap about when you walk. Accessorise your cowboy with a rugged, country-looking shirt and a handkerchief (red or blue if possible) tied around the neck.

Of course, the best cowboy role to be is the Sheriff, so you'll need a nice shiny badge. Cut a star shape out of some stiff cardboard. The most basic star is two equilateral (come on, remember third-year trig – 60° each

corner, sides of equal length!) triangles facing in
opposite directions one on top of the other.

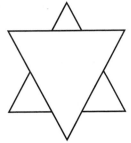

Cover the star with paper glue and wrap in
aluminium foil. You can try being really subtle
about it, and, before you get going with the glue,
use a blunt point and score the word 'Sheriff' into
the cardboard. When you smooth the foil over the
top, it should look like the word has been engraved
in metal. Or you can write it on in permanent marker afterwards. Stick a
safety pin to the back with some sellotape and assume a position of authority.

Pirate

To be an authentic pirate, you should look like you've been put on a spin
cycle in salt water for the best part of a year. 'Distressed' is a good word.

If you've got an old pair of dark-coloured trousers, cut them off a
couple of inches below the knee in a zig-zag pattern so they look torn and
a bit shipwrecked. Add a few tears around the thighs and knees.

Your average pirate held his trousers up with a bit of handy rigging, so
instead of a belt, tie a good thick bit of rope round your waist and make
sure it's got lots of shipshape knots in it. Alternatively, you could be a bit
flash and tie a nice red sash round your waist, but it depends if you've got
a long, wide bit of scarlet red cloth kicking around.

Any old T-Shirt will do, but avoid anything with a Tigger or Barbie
Princess motif. Typical piratey colours include blue and white stripes, red,
black, white or blue. Long or short sleeves depend on whether you're a pirate
of the Caribbean or Norwegian Fjord. Then, it's all in the accessorising.

Bandana: You'll need a big handkerchief or square of cloth, preferably
red or black for the bandana. Fold it in half so it makes a triangle and
put the longest side around your forehead. Tie at the back in a big knot.

Eye patch: Simply cut an eye-patch shape (trace round one lens on a pair of glasses but exaggerate the size if you're not sure) from light cardboard (trusty cereal box time again!) and colour black. Thread elastic, ribbon or thick cotton through the top of the patch and tie round the back of the head.

Cutlass: Any knife shape will do. Cut it out of stiff cardboard, colour the hilt and handle black, and cover the blade in kitchen foil. You could cover the tip in red nail varnish for a more threatening look.

Bling: I don't know why pirates spend so long looking for treasure. They seem to be covered head to toe in masses of gold jewellery already. A hooped earring is a nice touch, but difficult to keep on if you don't have the corresponding hole in your ear. Stick to a few bangles – you can make bangles and rings out of scrunched-up kitchen foil if you don't have any handy.

Knight

Find a piece of white cloth that when folded double reaches from the shoulders to halfway down the thighs, and comfortably covers the whole torso from one side to the other. An old sheet will do nicely. The tunic shape is a very simple rectangle folded in half. At the fold, cut a square hole big enough to get a head through.

Wear the tunic over black top and trousers (I'm not sure they had denim in ye olde days of the round table) and tie a belt around the middle. Try pinching one of Dad's ties and knot it loosely so it hangs down a bit.

Every knight needs a coat of arms. Design anything you fancy and draw it on a stiff piece of cardboard. The inside of a cereal packet is about the right size and thickness but you might want to put a layer of white paper on top as the inside of the boxes is a bit grey and uninspiring. Then glue or staple the coat of arms to the tunic.

Frankenstein

For Frankie, a lot of the effect is in the make-up, techniques for which are detailed on page 128. Black is the theme: Big black shoes – the clumpier the better – black trousers, black jumper and a black blazer.

Complement the look with a nice overall ashen face colour, with dark rings round the eyes, pale lips, some deep frown lines on the forehead and a scar or two on the cheekbones.

You will need to make Frankie's nuts. And bolts. Scrumple up some newspaper into a golf-ball-sized lump. Secure with some tape. Make a collar out of thick paper or thin card. Once you've decided on the colour of your face paint, try to make the collar a similar colour. Stick the balls onto opposite sides of the collar and draw a stitched scar pattern in between. Put round the neck and attach the ends together at the back with a bit of tape.

A gift

You'll need a fairly enormous box that will hold its shape well. If someone has recently had a piece of furniture or television delivered, these boxes are best. Alternatively, scout round local shops that may well have some spare.

Cut a hole in the top big enough for the head and one in each side at a comfortable height to get your arms through and still have some mobility. Cut the flaps off the bottom so you have space underneath to walk and get in and out of the box for those essential trips to the smallest room.

Wrap the whole box in gift paper appropriate for the occasion, i.e. birthday for a birthday, Christmas for Christmas etc. Unless you have a monster roll of paper, try to get the joins going vertically through the middle of the box. Then use some plain tissue or crepe paper to create a ribbon look round the middle. If you want to look really daft, save a length of the tissue to make a matching huge bow, that you can attach to your head using hair clips or another headband made from our trusty tights.

When nature calls, you may need to take the box off in public, so give a little thought to what you want to wear underneath. A leotard and some opaque tights are the bare minimum but anything light that won't show out the top or bottom will do.

Remember: while the bigger the box, the bigger the comedy value, a) the further your arms are from your mouth (you won't be able to drink anything) and b) the fewer doorways you'll be able to get through.

Dice

Follow the instructions for making a gift (see above), but instead of wrapping paper, use white paper or paint the box white. Then either paint on the black spots, or cut black circles out and glue them on. Remember for authenticity that all the opposing sides on a dice add up to seven.

Skeleton

Use a black sweatshirt or long-sleeved T-Shirt and black trousers as a base for your skeleton. To make the bones, use firmish card, such as the inside of a cereal box. You will need quite a few, though, to make enough clavicles and femurs. Also, you want your bones to be nice and white (cereal-box grey may be more true to life – or death – but it ain't as pretty) so stick a layer of white paper on top. Cut each set of bones out and stick them to the black outfit. It's handier to do this while there's a body in the clothes so you get a sense of where everything needs to go. Using staples at the ends of each bone rather than glueing them down makes the bones easy to remove at the end of the day without damaging the clothes too much.

For a good deathly look, use some white make-up or face paint to cover the whole of the face, and use black or dark grey eyeshadow to fill the eye sockets and cover the nose.

Dressing-up box

If you don't need a specific outfit, or the kids are driving you barmy on a rainy day, this is a handy box of tricks to keep adding to for impromptu catwalk shows or fantasy games.

You don't need anything special for a dressing-up box. Kids are endlessly fascinated by grown-ups' clothes. It's also a natural home for all those awful things you have lurking at the back of the wardrobe that cost too much just to be slung out or given to the charity shop.

If you simply can't part with anything in your collection then head off down the charity shop yourself, or conduct a raid on an even older generation's chest of drawers.

Ideal dressing-up items include:

- Hats – particularly with big brims or flowers
- Big coats
- Floaty dresses
- Old shirts – double up as painting smocks

- Trousers
- High-heeled shoes
- Uniforms
- Costume jewellery
- Evening outfits – long, formal gloves, bow ties, feather boas and sequins go down well
- Shawls
- Ski or sports gear

Making up isn't hard to do

You don't need to be a stage make-up artist with a panoply of pancake to add some special effects. You might want to stock up on some cheaper black eyeliner and black or grey eyeshadow, though. It would make my heart bleed to use half a stick of £20 designer lippy on the school play.

Ghosts, ghouls and the undead

You want the face as light as possible so instead of putting loose powder on top of foundation, use a light scattering of plain flour. A good trick for a real zombie face is one of those old-fashioned clay face packs. Make sure it isn't medicated or going to irritate the skin, then ladle it on good and thick and wait for it to dry. Then break into a big smile and really crack up.

Use a dark eyeshadow and work it all the way round the eye sockets. You just want a light suggestion of eyeshadow if the subject is supposed to be a bit peaky. For a skeleton, you want to go the whole hog and get it as black as possible. Add a bit on the nose and lips too.

Also, use dark eyeshadow instead of blusher to enhance the sunken-cheekbone look, blending it from the hairline into the face, tracing just underneath the cheekbone.

Swarthy and exotic characters

Pirates, devils, vampires and ancient anythings all need some subtle, but still important, making up. Generally, a bit of eyeliner and maybe a spot of bronzing powder if you have any to hand will do the trick. Make the eyeliner a bit more heavy-handed than an everyday look.

However, with your Ancient Egyptian character, you want to think big. Draw a normal eyeliner line across the top of the eye but, as you get to the outside corner, keep going for a good centimetre or so straight out towards the hairline. Then draw another, thicker line just above the original one, leaving the tiniest sliver of eyelid showing through. If you happen to have some electric-blue eyeshadow then, for extra dramatic effect, paint it over the remaining eyelid, right up to the eyebrow, which can also be 'coloured in' using the black eyeliner.

Scars and bruises

You're going to need a lot of black eyeliner by the end of all of this. Scars are pretty simple as we're not going for the genuine Hollywood effect here.

For scars like the one our Frankie needs (see page 125), simply draw a ragged line across the appropriate area, and then draw lots more little lines crossing it to make the stitches. Don't make them too even – you don't want to imply that they were sewn up by a professional.

Bruises are just a smudge of lots of different eyeshadows to create that sort of blue/black/red/green mottled effect. Concentrate the most shadow in the middle of the bruise, tapering out as you get to the edges. Smudge it in roughly with your finger, adding one colour on top of the other until you have mutilated your victim to your satisfaction.

Chapter Nine

Some party stuff

f course, there's absolutely no point being all dressed up with nowhere to go. If there's one thing kids' lives are full of, it's parties, parties, parties. And before you have to face the dreaded teen-alone house party, you have years of quaint party games, paper hats and cakes shaped like Barbie to 'enjoy'.

Party themes

No one really needs an excuse for a party. Does the day have a 'Y' in it? Hooray! Let's celebrate.

Mind you, kids have enough excuses for parties, they don't need to invent any more. Which is why, after so many 'turn up, play pass the parcel, eat cake, go home, be sick' events', you might want to shake it up a bit with a theme. Plus, you need a use for all the outfits in the previous chapter.

Having themed parties takes a little bit of thought, but who said you had to do the work. Get the kids roped into making the decorations and accessories. Instead of being a chore for them, it'll just prolong anticipation of the party.

Pirate theme

As well as the outfits (see page 123), you can have treasure maps – perhaps for the directions to the house on the invites. What about making small treasure chests instead of party bags to take home? Forget all the fancy bits and bobs in the party bag and just give lots of shiny chocolate money. Always a winner. Perhaps forfeits for losing the party games could include walking the plank? Change the Red Rover game into Pirates versus the East India Company (i.e. goodies *vs* baddies depending on your point of view).

Mediaeval theme

This is all about knights, sword fights and jousting. Obviously, horses are out of the question but how about getting competitors to stand on a bucket each and trying to bash each other off with pillows. Hide and seek becomes knights rescuing damsels in distress. If you're feeling really adventurous, how about rigging up a drawbridge to gain admittance to the party? If kids are of the age where they want to do more than sit in the back garden and play games, take the party down to a local archery centre. They're dotted all over the country and it'll look like the real Robin Hood deal when they're drawing back their bows.

Treasure Island theme

Again, use maps as invites. The dress code should be 'distressed' (see page 123) right down to beards (optional for both boys and girls). Team games include the most innovative way of writing a big 'Help!' sign on the ground. Or tying messages to balloons (helium-filled ones float further). Set a competition to make lunch with the only 'rations' that were swept up with the castaway (it will be helpful if the result is edible and doesn't need cooking – an exotic island fruit salad, for example).

Cowboys and Indians theme

You'll need lots of cowboy and Indian skills here. Making feather headdresses, sending smoke signals (you might want to fire up the BBQ), lassoing livestock (or perhaps a chair – you don't want to traumatise the family dog any more than you can help) are all good fun. There'll be lots of target practice because both parties are forever shooting at each other. Instead of real guns, however, try slingshots and tin cans on the fence. Or really simply, string an elastic band between your thumb and forefinger. Pull it back in the middle with the other hand, while positioning a small ball of paper in the middle. Let go of the middle of the band and the paper at the same time and it should shoot off. Maybe make paper targets of the 'enemy' to shoot at and soak the balls of paper in red paint for good 'splattage'.

Stars in their eyes theme

Time to unleash their inner diva. You could hire a real karaoke machine or simply get the CD player and let them sing along to some current number ones. Dress code is 'superstar'. Arrange into teams of judges and performers (let them swap so that everyone gets a go) and encourage the most 'out there' performances, along with spectacular put-downs (observe so it doesn't get too personal!). Have a big disco at the end so that everyone can burn off the cheesy Wotsits and have a good old boogie.

Halloween game – Treacle dookin'

We always played this in the Brownies at Halloween in Scotland, before we went out Guysing. Hang a row of drop scones, or Scotch pancakes that have been half-coated in treacle, from a length of string at just about head height. Then prepare a washing-up bowl full of water with lots of apples bobbing in it. Then follow that with another slightly smaller (but still big enough to get the average head in) bowl filled with flour and chocolate money.

Do this twice for two teams, lined up next to each other. The first person has to run down the line of pancakes and take a big bite out of one and swallow it, before running to the apples and, using only their teeth and not their hands, take one out of the bowl, and then run onto the flour and take out a coin. By the end, each player is covered in a treacly, wet, floury mess.

You can't progress to the next bowl if you haven't succeeded at the last, so each player must bite a pancake, an apple and a coin before the next can set off. The winning team is the one with all players back at the start first.

You might want to play this one towards the end of the evening as it has a habit of ruining the Halloween make-up, along with much of the top half of the outfit.

Halloween theme

Obviously, you can do ghosts and ghouls at any time but 31 October is the natural day for spooky happenings. Make some silly slime (see page 54) for a gross part of the going-home present. Keep icing and other food to tasteful colour schemes such as green, red and black. Tell spooky stories with the lights out. Decorate with black bats and silver thread for cobwebs, as well as lots of lit pumpkins. Scoop out all the flesh of the pumpkin and cut some scary faces in the front. A Stanley knife does the job well. Pop a tealight inside to illuminate.

Party Games

A party's just not a party without some traditional games. They're even played well into adulthood, although admittedly with more than a small injection of alcohol.

Pass the parcel

This classic birthday party game is a great one to kick off festivities. Sitting in a circle, kids pass round a very well wrapped-up present until the music stops. The person holding the present tears off a layer of paper and the music begins again, starting the passing again. It keeps going until someone unwraps the last layer and reveals the gift, which they then get to keep.

Top tip: Don't waste lots of pretty paper in wrapping. Newspaper is fine. Also, it's not going to go five rounds with the Royal Mail so keep the sellotape to a minimum. It's all about getting one layer down, not trying to find out what's underneath.

Pin the tail on the donkey

Don't try this on a real donkey. Draw a child-sized picture of a donkey, or any other animal or human you feel it might be amusing to stick a sharp pin in.

On a piece of card (you guessed, an old cereal box does nicely), cut out a shape that would be fun to pin on the donkey. A tail, a hat, a cake, a tennis racket or a wooden spoon are all useful.

Each child takes turns to put on a blindfold and stick the 'tail' or other item where they think it should be. The closest to the correct place wins but you could also praise those with the best comedy value.

Variation: You can create a different object for each child, and keep them all blindfolded until all the items have been pinned on. Then you can reveal the ridiculous picture that you've created.

Blind man's buff

Getting value for money from our blindfolds, you can follow pin the tail on the donkey with a quick go at blind man's buff. One person is 'it' and wears the blindfold. The others dart around the blind man, trying not to get caught. There are two versions of this game. In one, the group is confined in a small area and simply try to avoid capture. If they are hugged by the blind man, they're out. In the other version, they don't have to avoid being touched, but if they are they have to stand still while the blind man feels their face and shoulders and tries to guess who they are. If he guesses correctly, the person is out. If not, the game continues. Last person left wins and becomes the blind man.

Famous faces

This kiddie version of a drinking game is great to play while everyone is sitting down and guzzling, as it provides temporary relief from inhaling crisps. Someone starts by thinking of a famous person's name. The person on their left has to think of someone famous whose first name begins with the first letter of the surname of the name last mentioned. Still with me? So, if someone starts with Cary Grant, the next person has to come up with a 'G' – George Michael, for example. If the person manages to think of someone whose first and last names begin with the same letter, the direction of play reverses, until someone does the same thing again. If a famous name is repeated, then the person is out. Keep going until you run out of names.

Treasure hunt

Simple concept: hide a series of clues around the house and garden, which lead to a prize. You can be as simple or as creative as you like with this one. Clues should be pretty easy – you want to make it a challenge but you don't want to find a stray child hunting in the airing cupboard at 3 a.m. either.

You can have a free for all but I've found that you need an awful lot of clues to keep everyone interested. Two teams work best. Two sets of clues, on two different colours of paper, leading in two different directions, for two different prizes.

It works really well in the garden as an after-food activity because it burns off the cheesy straws and gets them out of the way so you can begin to get some of the chaos cleared away. That said, as long as you don't lead them anywhere you don't want them to be, it works just fine in the house too.

Here are some generic clues you can use for the average garden and house:

Garden

- If I took a leaf out of his book then I would have to branch out in a different direction (tree)
- This place sheds some light on the problem (shed)
- If you think this clue is a load of rubbish, wait till you find the next one! (bin – you might want to make sure it's empty first)
- Sometimes it feels like I've been hung out to dry (washing line)
- If I plant this idea in your head, a girl's name will begin to flower (daisy, iris, poppy etc. – I didn't say they might not need your help sometimes!)
- Your quest might be a pot of gold, but I think your plans are all to pot! (empty garden pot where you can hide the spoils)

Generally, the bigger or more intricate your garden, the fewer clues you'll need as they take longer to be found. And vice versa, small empty garden, more and more complicated clues.

House

- It'll all come out in the wash (obvious clue but don't put it in the obvious place – instead of the washing-machine drum, put it in the soap dispenser, or even in the soap itself)

- You've got mail (knowing this generation, they'll rush to the computer. Confuse them and trap the next clue in the letterbox!)
- I'm feeling flushed with success so far (toilet or bathroom)
- I must be green-fingered to get this far – are you planting ideas in my head? (pot plant)
- What a lot of old rubbish these clues are (bin)
- If you don't find the prize here, how will I cushion the blow? (sofa or armchair)

At then end, because it's a treasure hunt, you could have a pot of gold (a tub of chocolate coins in a gold-coloured box) for team A, and a casket of jewels (boiled fruit sweets or jelly beans in a box wrapped in silver foil) for team B. It doesn't really matter which team wins as there's no extra prize, but there's a certain smugness to being first.

Hide and seek/sardines

What's to explain about hide and seek? One person is 'It', they count to 10, 20 or 100 depending on how many have to hide, how old they are and how many spaces there are to hide. Then they shout good and loud, 'Coming, ready or not!' Last person found becomes 'it' and you keep going until everyone's had a go, got bored or run out of time.

If this is a bit old hat, try sardines. This time, only one person goes off to hide and everyone else counts. Then they all split up to find the person. Once someone finds the person hiding, they join them in the hiding place. As each one finds the growing group of people, they join in. The last person to find the now enormous pile of squashed people (hence, sardines) has to go off and hide for the next round.

After both games, it's always worthwhile doing a bit of a headcount, just in case you find a sardine has joined the treasure hunter in the airing cupboard.

Charades

This is a simple mime and guessing game, but you might want to mug up on the culture of your target age group to help get the guessing going. Demonstrate some of the clues such as film, song, play and book. Syllables might be beyond the younger age group, but number of words is fine. Other helpful signs are the 'T' for 'the' and moving thumb and forefinger together for 'little word' or 'smaller'.

Let the audience shout out guesses but keep an eye out for the one who gets it right, as it's their turn next. This can keep going for as long as you want it to and is handy for the end of a party as it doesn't matter if you lose players halfway through.

Who Am I?/Rizla game

Who am I?, better known among grown-ups as the Rizla game, this can be played just as well with Post-it notes and even masking tape. Every player selects either a job, an animal or a famous person for another player. They secretly write this down on the Post-it note and stick it either to their victim's back or forehead. So everyone has a sticker attached to them.

Then everyone mills about asking questions of everyone else about the thing they are supposed to be. The catch is that you are only allowed to ask each person one question – so it better be a goodie – and you are only allowed to answer 'yes' or 'no'. The first person to stick up their hand and guess what or who they are is the winner. If they get it wrong, they can't ask questions for 10 seconds.

Simon says ...

A classic game to get everyone warmed up and in the mood to be silly. The caller faces the group and calls, 'Simon says ... stand on one leg.' Everyone must copy and keep doing whatever Simon says until Simon changes his mind and says something else. 'Simon says ... hop like a bunny' and so on. Every now and again, give an order without including 'Simon says ...' and if anyone follows the order, they're out! Equally, if Simon says something and they don't follow the order, or get it wrong, they're out too.

Red Rover

Divide players into two teams. Each team forms a line by holding hands and stretching themselves out. The two teams stand 25ft apart or more facing each other. Each side takes turns calling, 'Red Rover, Red Rover, send [name] right over.' At that signal, the player called, runs from his line and tries to break through the line of his/her opponents. If he breaks through, he can take one opponent back with him to his team. If he does not break through, he joins the other team. The team to add the most players wins.

Musical chairs

Put out two rows of chairs, back to back, with one chair for each child, minus one. When the music starts playing, the children have to skip round the rows of chairs. When the music stops, each child has to race to find a seat. The one without a seat is out of the game.

The round starts again but another chair is taken away. This continues until there is only one chair left, and two contestants. The one left sitting when the music stops wins.

You can heighten the anticipation by alternating how long you play the music for each round, and by 'faking' hitting the pause button. If you get cheats who try to 'hog' a chair by not dancing round fairly, you can make them stand a few paces to the side of the dance, and then they have further to race to get to one of the remaining chairs when the music stops.

Musical statues

A similar concept to musical chairs, but this time when the music stops everyone has to stand stock still. The first to flinch is out but joins the music master in spotting movers next time. They are joined each round by more and more flinchers. If everyone is managing to stand very still for a long time, start the music again to get them moving. The game ends with most of the 'out' players trying to make one of the remaining two twitch by pulling funny faces or clapping their hands very close to the statue's face. The watchers aren't allowed to touch the statues. Last to stand still wins.

Balloon bust relay

Separate into two teams. Blow up one balloon for each member of the team, preferably using different colours for each team. Make them nice and tight so that they should burst relatively easily under pressure. Each team lines up at one end of the room, the balloons are lined up on the floor at the other end.

On 'get set ... go', each member takes it in turn to run up to the first inflated balloon and lies on it to pop it. They mustn't pop it with their hands, feet or teeth. When it's popped, they run back to their team and tag the next one to go. No team member can run back until their balloon has been popped. The winning team is the one that has all its members back in line after popping all the balloons.

Variation: If there are enough members of the team, and frankly you can be bothered, before you blow up the balloons, you can put a piece of paper inside. These can say anything you like, but should make sense when the team reads them out one after the other.

For example, a team of eight kids could each get a piece of paper that says:

Fish – swim – in – pink – sea – but – elephants – don't

They only win if they pop all the balloons, pick up the bit of paper and then as a team read it all out in the right order once the last member has returned to the line.

Top tip: To stop the balloons disappearing all over the place, it helps to staple the knotted end to a square about 10cm x 10cm of heavyish cardboard.

The shivering spoon

Another two-team relay, with an added frisson. A few hours before the party, put two big metal spoons (serving spoons are good) in the freezer. Tape a long piece of string to the spoon handle – about 3m is long enough for a team of five players. Increase it by a metre for every two players more.

Hand the cold spoons to the heads of the team just before shouting, 'Go!' The first member of the team has to pass the spoon down the inside of their top and out the bottom and hand it to the next person. They then thread the spoon up the inside of their top from bottom to top. This pattern is repeated down the line until the last person has got the spoon out and holds it up in the air. The teams are then completely tied together. They then race the spoon back to the beginning again, untying themselves.

Variation: You can turn this into a multiple version of the three-legged race by getting the tied-together team to run round the garden and back before undoing themselves.

The chocolate game

Everyone sits in a circle with a pile of heavy winter clothes in the middle, a mega-size block of chocolate open on a paper plate, a knife and fork. When the music starts you pass around a tennis ball, or a cup – anything easily held that won't get in the way.

When the music stops, the person holding the object dashes into the middle of the circle and puts on all the items of clothing. Once they're wearing everything, then they are allowed to use the knife and fork to cut off a square of chocolate. They may eat the square of chocolate only if they can get it to their mouth using the knife and fork. When the music starts again, they must stop wherever they are (even if the chocolate is tantalisingly close to their mouth) and take off all the clothes as quickly as possible to rejoin the circle.

It takes around 30 seconds to get all the clothes on and then cut off a bit of chocolate. The person stopping and starting the music should aim to give them at least this much time to get going. To prevent any calls of 'not fair', the music master might want to face away from the circle so they can't see how the person eating the chocolate is getting on, thus preventing them from starting the music again just as the eater has got the final glove on.

The music starts and stops for as long as there is any chocolate, or a good few people have had a go. Getting towards the end, you can spice it up a bit by stopping the music again before the last person has had a chance to get all the clothes off, resulting in a bit of a tussle for the gloves as the next one waits to get at the chocolate.

In the end, divide the remaining chocolate up among all the players so they all get at least one bit in the end. Ahhh, I do like happy endings.

Party food

Where kids are involved, party food should be simple, cheap and buffet style. The last thing you want to try to do is turn out 30 cooked and plated meals within seconds of each other. Leave that to Gordon Ramsay.

Pile it all on a big table in various bowls and plates and let them help themselves. Yes, the first choice will be the crisps, yes, their eyes will be bigger than their stomachs and, yes, there will be a lot of mess and leftovers. I suggest you invest in a big paper tablecloth and paper plates and when it's all over scoop it all up in one big Dick Whittington-type parcel and chuck it in the bin.

Children can be fussy so don't be surprised if they turn their noses up at gourmet hors d'oeuvres. Even if they eat organic tahini the rest of the time, this is also a party so crack out the cheesy Wotsits and white bread.

Be aware of any allergies and exclude that type of food completely. Segregating it doesn't work as the slightest contamination can cause a reaction.

A suggested children's party menu is:

'Real' food:

Pizza squares
Cheese sandwiches
Tuna mayonnaise sandwiches
Ham sandwiches
Pork pies
Scotch eggs
Quiche slices
Cocktail sausages

'Snack' stuff

Cheesy puffs
Ready salted crisps (you can get reduced-salt versions)
Rice cakes
Bread sticks

'Healthy' snack stuff

Sticks of celery
Chopped peppers
Chopped carrots
Chopped cucumber
Dips – taramasalata, houmous, cheese, thousand island

Puddings

Trifle
Biscuits
Fruit salad
Birthday cake!

Drinks

Squash (avoid orange if you can, it's got all those e-numbers that send kids bonkers)
Fruit juice
Still and sparkling water

Now, you don't have to give them everything from the above, a couple from each list will be more than sufficient. And if you're worried that it's all junk – well, you can make your own pizza very healthily. Ditto quiche. Replace cheapo cocktail sausages with chopped-up organic normal ones and keep the snacks to a minimum.

But remember – it's a PARTY! Go on, spoil 'em. You can send them to fat camp later.

The birthday party – a survival guide

1   **Keep them calm:** Whether your child is the star of the show, or just going to bask in someone else's glory, you don't want to get them all wound up or tired before the big event. Keep excitement and e-numbers to a minimum or you'll end up with a cranky monster. There'll be plenty of time for mega-tantrums after they've been jammed full of chocolate and crisps.

   Even if the party food fills in for lunch, it's worthwhile trying to get a healthy snack down kids beforehand. It will hopefully limit the damage from all the sugar and excitement, and may make them just full enough to prevent cheesy-twist overdose.

2   **Confine the chaos:** Try to keep all the games and food in one room, then the rest of your house remains useable and you can always shut the door for a couple of days if you can't face the aftermath quite yet. Ideally, though, you'll want a big space to eat, and enough space to play party games for little ones, or have a disco for the older ones. This may mean spilling over into another room, or, if the weather's good, the garden. Whatever space you use, cover floors and, in the case of the grafitti party (see page 209), walls to minimise fall-out.

3 **Food:** Now is not the time for organic, salt-reduced, wholemeal bread with tahini. Push the junk boat out – it's more fun and generally a lot cheaper. That said, you can squeeze in stuff that grew out of the ground instead of a test tube, as long as you pretty it up a bit. For finger food, batons of carrots, red peppers, cucumber, celery and anything else that can be chopped up stick-shaped and dipped will do the job nicely. See page 144 for some sample nosh.

4 **Entertainers:** A word about Bobo the Clown. If you can avoid it, don't bother with hiring entertainers. They're pricey and at least one precocious little beggar will decide he's above it all and heckle. Plus, problem party kids come in pairs. At the other end of the scale, there'll be a shy, retiring violet who's utterly terrified of grown men in make-up and will scream inconsolably for hours. 'Entertainers' also mean that instead of running around and burning off all the refined sugar, the kids get numb-bummed and twitchy.

5 **Timing:** The best time of day to hold a party is late lunchtime as half the fun is the anticipation. Invitees can spend the morning looking for the perfect gift and sorting out the party outfit, while the guest of honour can supervise final adjustments to the decorations and food.

The average kid's party feels like it lasts an eternity, so you may be surprised to discover that the maximum length is about two hours. With all the eating, present opening and running around required, that may seem barely enough but trust me, it's plenty.

6 **Running order:** It sounds churlish to regiment something as innocent as a kid's party, but you will need structure unless you want full-scale anarchy.

Start by impressing upon parents that activities will begin promptly and if they don't want their beloved to miss out, they should get there on time. Anticipate early partygoers by sticking a DVD on in another room and offering some juice to tide them over. When 75% have arrived, get going.

When guests arrive, get them in, take coats and allow the star of the show to open each gift straight away. There are three reasons for this. It means the birthday boy or girl thank the giver personally; you can beam gratefully at the paying parent and they can beam proudly back; and it reduces the potential for embarrassment in a big opening extravaganza as the bringer of the multipack of pens from Tesco finds themselves hopelessly outclassed.

Kick off with a few friendly games where they're all in one place, such as pass the parcel or musical statues. Then, when they're warmed up, you could try getting a bit more energetic with musical chairs, Simon says ... or, if outdoors, Red Rover (see page 140).

When they've worked up a bit of an appetite, but are still all speaking to each other, it's time for some food. Buffet style is best but if you can fit them all sitting down at a table then that helps confine the mess. Otherwise, arrange for a space where they can bring their food and drinks to sit without risking spillage.

As sure as night follows day, birthday cake follows food. Get candles lit, enlist a couple of helpers to close curtains if it's too bright to make an impact and start a rousing version of 'Happy Birthday'.

And, oh, isn't it a great wheeze to have magic candles ... Look, he's blown them out – *Oh, no, he hasn't!* It's not so funny when you discover they burn 10 times faster than normal candles, spill wax all over the icing, have a flame 10ft tall and are impossible to extinguish without throwing the whole thing in the sink. Stick to normal candles.

After food, it's time for more activity, usually the 'big game'. If it's possible to get outside, do. The 'big game' is something like a treasure hunt (see page 136) or hide and seek (see page 138), which goes on longer than musical statues, and has a beginning, middle and an end.

When you have a winner from your 'big game', it's time to cool things down a bit with some gentler games such as Who am I? or charades (see page 139). Charades can pretty much go on indefinitely and it's a good one to play while parents arrive as it doesn't matter if you gradually lose players.

Hand out party bags as kids go off one by one. It's a nice way of bringing them down gently and they finally 'win' something if they've been really crap at all the other games.

7   **The party bag:** I hate competitive parenting even more than you. It gets no more competitive than kids' parties. One of the worst offenders is the party bag. It's not unusual for kids to come back from a party with a brand-new fancy dress outfit, a new toy, a colossal bag of sweets, stationery, CDs, DVDs, cameras and anything else you can imagine. This has got to stop.

Along with my embargo on Bobo the Clown, I'm issuing a moratorium on party bags that wouldn't look out of place at the Oscars. This, as far as I'm concerned, is the ultimate party bag:

1 slice of birthday cake, preferably a bit squashed onto a paper napkin
1 thank-you card personally written days before the event
1 noise maker (no, not an iPod; a plastic whistle or a kazoo, if you're really pushing the boat out)
1 novelty pen
1 small novelty notepad
1 handful of sweeties
1 balloon (uninflated)
1 novelty keyring

And that's *it*! Most supermarkets now sell multipacks of party bag-type stuff. Much as I hate useless tat, kids love it and it keeps costs down. When you've got around 20 kids to provide for, you don't want the bag costing more than one or two quid per child.

You even have the opportunity to make your own party bag contents that are cheap as chips. Take the playdough recipe from the craft section (see page 41) and some freezer bags and make up playdough kits to take home. Making hard playdough models is a great activity for younger party animals, and if you get them going on it the moment they arrive, you have time to stick them in the oven to harden before it's time to go home. That way they can take their model (and some more kit to make another one) home with them to keep the fun going.

8   **Cleaning up:** By this point, the last thing you want to think about is cleaning. The only thing on your mind is that enormous bottle of gin that's been calling your name every time you went into the kitchen for more jugs of orange squash. However, a couple of tips to ease the pain:

- Use paper cups and plates – they're not environmentally friendly but they can go in the recycling if you feel very guilty.
- Don't save leftovers. It's horrid kiddy party food. You will not thank yourself for hanging on to several bowls of cheesy puffs and half a trifle (it's not even got any sherry in it – chuck it all in the bin).
- Bin the decorations too. You may have been up until 1 a.m. making dangly mobiles and paper chains but by next year they'll look tatty and Junior will demand something different anyway. In the bin they go.

9   **Relax:** Until next year.

Chapter Ten

Some small stuff

nce you get the hang of all the technical stuff, babies and toddlers aren't hard to keep happy. But proper research with scientific doctors in white coats suggests that it's not completely healthy to leave them in front of the TV for hours at a stretch. It's probably helpful to have a couple of ideas up your sleeve for those moments in between eating, sleeping and pooing when they need a bit of soothing and entertaining.

Fortunately, despite appearances to the contrary in most kiddie-kit shops, you don't need a lot of apparatus to hold onto your sanity when dealing with the under-threes.

Newborns–6 months: Big, bold picture shapes, preferably in black and white, work well for newborns. Colourful pictures of animals and objects and things that dangle and spin are favourites as they get older.

Photocopy some black-and-white spirals and stick them up where your baby can see them. Scrunch up some aluminium foil and hang it from a mobile. Make sure your baby can't reach the mobile to pull the balls off because they can be a choking hazard. They start teething at around 5–6 months and are always chewing and sticking things in their mouths.

6 months–1 year: Crawling, cruising and even walking happen around now, and all this new-found mobility just increases their curiosity. Every cupboard holds a new fascination, which is why mums make dads spend their weekends child-proofing the house.

Try leaving access to one floor-level cupboard to satisfy their curiosity. Remove any jammed finger potential by sticking a big lump of plasticine or Blu-tack to the top corner (out of reach of little fingers) of the cupboard so it won't close fully. Leave some unbreakable plates and cups and other objects that small hands can explore. They also love making noise so leave a wooden spoon and a pan in there for plenty banging potential.

1–2 years: By the time they hit one year old, new toddlers will have found a whole new toy to play with. Two in fact: their feet. Whoever coined the phrase, 'Don't run before you can walk,' obviously never had small children. Once they make it past three consecutive steps, they seem to want to tear everywhere. Give them the opportunity to put their new skills to the test by playing gentle football or running races outside. **Bonus:** They're still having at least one nap a day at this point so the more time spent running around outside in the morning, the more time it buys you mid-afternoon while they sleep it off.

Obsessions: At this age, littlies will often fixate on one thing: dollies, trains, lorries, cats. They'll be happy with anything that relates to their passion. Pictures, films, objects, even just a basic pen drawing will make them happy. Even at this tender age, the Internet is your friend. Google Images and Video have something for almost everyone.

2–3 years: Anything that involves making a righteous mess goes down well with toddlers. Messy play can mean finger painting, sandpits, making mud pies, digging holes or simply splashing in puddles.

You don't need any special equipment for playing with water. Just fill up a bath and fill with bits of Tupperware and old washing-up liquid bottles. Tubs can be boats and lids can be rafts. Try to get as many (waterproof) toys to float on a raft before you sink it.

If the bath is next to a wall, draw a simple paper target and use the water bottles to try to hit it. You could pin up a few. The traditional circles are a bit tricky and complex so try sticking up pictures of a duck, a bus, PC Plod – simple shapes they'll recognise and will find funny hitting with a blast of water.

This is also typically the age when kids turn into stubborn little beggars when it comes to bathtime, so if they associate it with the place they play pirate ships then you might have it easier at the end of the day.

Sing for your supper

When my son was born, I panicked. I could manage the nappies, sleepless nights were no biggie and he seemed to survive regardless how much or little I managed to feed him. But could I remember one nursery rhyme or lullaby? Surely, I thought, the very essence of yummy mumminess is singing lullabies. 'Bohemian Rhapsody', I fear, just isn't a good enough substitute.

I could just about get most of the way through 'Baa, Baa, Black Sheep' and 'Twinkle, Twinkle, Little Star' but that was the extent of my repertoire. At toddler groups, I mimed along like a member of a bad-girl group. Hubby was on hand to help out with the bedtime singing but he's Welsh and all his lullabies were in some funny language that involved an excessive use of the letter 'L'. So if you're as useless as me, here are the words!

Songs for bedtime

The most typical tiddler song is the lullaby. The idea is that by singing sweetly you should be able to get the nippers to drop off to sleep without a peep. If only that were the case. However, lullabies genuinely have a soothing effect, and you don't need to be Pavarotti to get a good tune out. Even if all you can manage is a gentle hum, it's better than nothing.

Hush, little baby

Hush, little baby, don't say a word.
Papa's gonna buy you a mockingbird

And if that mockingbird won't sing,
Papa's gonna buy you a diamond ring

And if that diamond ring turns brass,
Papa's gonna buy you a looking glass

And if that looking glass gets broke,
Papa's gonna buy you a billy goat

And if that billy goat won't pull,
Papa's gonna buy you a cart and bull

And if that cart and bull fall down,
You'll still be the sweetest little baby in town.

Rock a-bye, baby

Rock-a-bye, baby,
On the treetop,
When the wind blows
The cradle will rock;
When the bough breaks
The cradle will fall,
And down will come baby,
Cradle and all.

Baby is drowsing,
Cosy and fair.

Mother sits near,
In her rocking chair.
Forward and back
The cradle she swings,
And though baby sleeps,
He hears what she sings.

From the high rooftops
Down to the sea,
No one's as dear
As baby to me.
Wee little fingers,
Eyes wide and bright --
Now sound asleep
Until morning light.

Baa, baa, black sheep

Baa, baa, black sheep,
Have you any wool?
Yes sir, yes sir,
Three bags full.

One for the master,
One for the dame,
And one for the little boy
Who lives down the lane.

Baa, baa, black sheep,
Have you any wool?
Yes sir, yes sir,
Three bags full.

Action songs

Of course, not all songs for little ones need have a sedative effect (although I guess it depends how long you spend with them each day). Toddlers love copying and dancing, and giving them songs to do actions to keeps them amused for ages. It's also something you can do anywhere, provided you aren't easily embarrassed.

Wheels on the bus

The wheels on the bus go round and round *(and so do your arms)*
Round and round, round and round
The wheels on the bus go round and round
All day long

The wipers on the bus go 'Swish, swish, swish, *(and so do your arms, again)*
Swish, swish, swish, swish, swish, swish'
The wipers on the bus go 'Swish, swish, swish'
All day long

The horn on the bus goes 'Beep, beep, beep *(place finger on nose)*
Beep, beep, beep, beep, beep, beep'
The horn on the bus goes 'Beep, beep, beep'
All day long

The children on the bus go chitter chatter chitter *(open and close*
    fingers)
Chitter chatter chitter
Chitter chatter chitter
The children on the bus go chitter chatter chitter
All day long

The driver of the bus goes, 'Quiet in the back!' *(finger to lips in*
    'shusshing' motion)
'Quiet in the back!
'Quiet in the back!'
The driver of the bus goes, 'Quiet in the back!'
All day long.

Incy Wincy Spider

Incy Wincy Spider
Climbed up the water spout *(fingers 'crawl' up an arm)*
Down came the rain *(fingers tap, tap, tap back down again)*
And washed the spider out
Out came the sun *(palm of the hand gently rubbing circles as*
    if to dry)
And dried up all the rain
And Incy Wincy Spider
Climbed up the spout again! *(fingers run up the arm and tickle*
    under the chin)

Hickory Dickory Dock

Tick, tock, tick, tock, tick, tock, tick *(waggle index fingers like a pendulum)*

Hickory Dickory Dock,
The mouse ran up the clock, *(fingers run up an imaginary clock)*
The clock struck one *(clap once, loudly)*
The mouse ran down, *(fingers run down again)*
Hickory Dickory Dock.

Tick-tock, tick tock *(pendulum fingers again)*

Hickory Dickory Dock,
The mouse ran up the clock,
The clock struck two *(clap twice, loudly)*
The mouse went, '*Boo!*'
Hickory Dickory Dock.
Tick-tock, tick tock

Hickory Dickory Dock,
The mouse ran up the clock,
The clock struck three *(three claps)*
The mouse went, '*Wheee!*' *(bring hands down into lap quickly)*
Hickory Dickory Dock.

Tick-tock, tick tock

Hickory Dickory Dock,
The mouse ran up the clock,
The clock struck four, *(four claps)*
The mouse said, '*No more!*' *(hold hands out in empty gesture)*
Hickory Dickory Dock.

Heads, shoulders, knees and toes

Head, shoulders, knees and toes, knees and toes, *(touch each bit as you sing)*

Head, shoulders, knees and toes, knees and toes,

And eyes and ears and mouth and nose,

Head, shoulders, knees and toes, knees and toes.

Repeat, missing out a body part every time you repeat the verse and replacing it with a 'hum'. By the end you should be just humming the whole song. Do one final verse but go as fast as you can.

Miss Polly had a dolly

Miss Polly had a dolly

Who was sick, sick, sick, *(rock the dolly)*

So she called for the doctor *(dial a telephone)*

To come quick, quick, quick; *(beckon to come quickly)*

The doctor came

With his bag and his hat, *(motion picking up bag, putting on hat)*

And he knocked on the door

With a rat-a-tat-tat. *(Knocking at the door)*

He looked at the dolly

And he shook his head, *(shake your head)*

He said, 'Miss Polly,

Put her straight to bed. *(wag your finger as if telling off)*

He wrote on a paper

For a pill, pill, pill, *(popping imaginary pill in mouth)*

'I'll be back in the morning

With my bill, bill, bill.' *(scribble on imaginary pad)*

Open, shut them

Open, shut them. *(holding arms out, open and close fists)*
Open, shut them.
Give a little clap. *(go on then!)*

Open, shut them
Put them in your lap. *(fold them in your lap)*
Creep them, creep them
Slowly creep them *(walk fingers up from tummy to your face)*
Right up to your chin
Open up your mouth *(so far, so good ...)*
But do not let them in. *(then suddenly clamp your mouth shut just
before the fingers get in)*

Songs for the heck of it!

These are great for car journeys because (thanks to this book) everyone
knows the words and the words are simple enough for most toddlers to be
able to join in after a while, even if they're only mimicking the sounds.

Daddy wouldn't buy me a bow-wow-wow

Daddy wouldn't buy for me a bow-wow, bow-wow,
Daddy wouldn't buy for me a bow-wow-wow!
I've got a little cat,
I suppose I'm fond of that,
But I'd rather have a bow-wow-wow!

The Wee Kirkcudbright Centipede
(Matt McGinn)

This is one of my favourite songs from my childhood, being a wee Scottish lass and all. You might want to track down the tune on the Internet, but any sing-song voice will do. And for the linguistically challenged among you, Kirkcudbright is pronounced 'Kir-koo-bree'.

Oh, the wee Kirkcudbright Centipede, oh, she was very sweet
She was very proud of every one of her hundred feet
Early every morning, her neighbours came to glance
She always entertained them with a beautiful little dance.

Chorus
As leg number 94 gave 95 a shunt
Legs number 1 and 2 were twisted out in front
Legs number 9 and 10 came wriggling up the side
73 and 74 were doing the parlor glide.

Now her neighbour, Jenny Longlegs, with jealousy was mad
She went out and bought herself a pencil and a pad
She came to look one morning, she made a careful note
Of every step the centipede made and this is what she wrote:

Chorus [substitute Well for As]

Now with her exact notations, little Jenny Longlegs tried
To dance just like the centipede, she failed and nearly cried
She grabbed hold of the centipede, and said, 'Now have a look,
Show me how to do this dance I've written in my book.'

[no chorus]

The centipede said, 'Do I do that?' tried to demonstrate
She hadn't thought it out before, and didn't do too great
Her hundred feet got twisted and she wound up in a tangle
She fractured 14 kneecaps, 7 shinbones and an ankle.

Chorus [this verse only]

As legs number 1 and 2 were tied with 3 and 4
Legs number 5 and 6 were canceled on the floor
Leg number 17 was attacked by number 10
98 and 99 will never dance again.

Oh, the wee Kirkcudbright Centipede she suffered in terrible pain
And all the bugs were very surprised the day she danced again
And now she tells her neighbours, anyone who comes to see,
'Never try an explanation of what comes naturally!'

Chorus

A hunting we will go

A hunting we will go, a hunting we will go
Heigh ho, the dairy-o, a hunting we will go
A hunting we will go, a hunting we will go
We'll catch a fox and put him in a box
And then we'll let him go

A hunting we will go, a hunting we will go
Heigh ho, the dairy-o, a hunting we will go
A hunting we will go, a hunting we will go
We'll catch a fish and put him on a dish
And then we'll let him go

A hunting we will go, a hunting we will go
Heigh ho, the dairy-o, a hunting we will go
A hunting we will go, a hunting we will go
We'll catch a bear and cut his hair
And then we'll let him go

A hunting we will go, a hunting we will go
Heigh ho, the dairy-o, a hunting we will go
A hunting we will go, a hunting we will go
We'll catch a pig and dance a little jig
And then we'll let him go

A hunting we will go, a hunting we will go
Heigh ho, the dairy-o, a hunting we will go
A hunting we will go, a hunting we will go
We'll catch a giraffe and make him laugh
And then we'll let him go

This old man

This old man, he played one,
He played knick-knack on my thumb;
Knick-knack paddywack,
Give a dog a bone,
This old man came rolling home.

This old man, he played two,
He played knick-knack on my shoe;
Knick-knack paddywhack,
Give a dog a bone,
This old man came rolling home.
This old man, he played three,
He played knick-knack on my knee;

Knick-knack paddywhack,
Give a dog a bone,
This old man came rolling home.

This old man, he played four,
He played knick-knack on my door;
Knick-knack paddywhack,
Give a dog a bone,
This old man came rolling home.

This old man, he played five,
He played knick-knack on my hive;
Knick-knack paddywhack,
Give a dog a bone,
This old man came rolling home.

This old man, he played six,
He played knick-knack on my sticks;
Knick-knack paddywhack,
Give a dog a bone,
This old man came rolling home.

This old man, he played seven,
He played knick-knack up in Heaven;
Knick-knack paddywhack,
Give a dog a bone,
This old man came rolling home.

This old man, he played eight,
He played knick-knack on my gate;
Knick-knack paddywhack,
Give a dog a bone,
This old man came rolling home.

This old man, he played nine,
He played knick-knack on my spine;
Knick-knack paddywhack,
Give a dog a bone,
This old man came rolling home.

This old man, he played ten,
He played knick-knack once again;
Knick-knack paddywhack,
Give a dog a bone,
This old man came rolling home.

Dance to your daddy

Dance to your daddy,
My little babby,
Dance to your daddy,
My little lamb!

You shall have a fishy
In a little dishy,
You shall have a fishy
When the boat comes in.

Dance to your daddy,
My little babby,
Dance to your daddy,
My little lamb;

You shall have an apple,
You shall have a plum,
You shall have a rattle-basket,
When your dad comes home.

Driving songs

As in 'driving Dad mad' songs, these are the sort of songs you want to sing when Dad's (ideally alone) in the car with the little cherubs. They're easy to remember, the melody's fairly basic and they last for a good long while. They can also drive the sanest person to murder.

99 bottles

99 bottles of beer on the wall
99 bottles of beer
Take one down, pass it around
98 bottles of beer on the wall

98 bottles of beer on the wall
98 bottles of beer
Take one down, pass it around
97 bottles of beer on the wall

Here's a song ...

Here's a song that'll get on your nerves
Get on your nerves
Get on your nerves
Here's a song that'll get on your nerves
And this is how it goes:

Here's a song that'll get on your nerves
Get on your nerves
Get on your nerves
Here's a song that'll get on your nerves
And this is how it goes:

[keep going until you get thrown out at Cherwell Valley Services]

Naughty songs

Itsy bitsys and wiggly worms can start to have a detrimental effect on your sanity after a while. You need a couple of songs in your repertoire that will keep the little ones happy, but let you snigger at the in-joke.

Beware though: Once old enough, they will figure it out and take great delight in giving a rousing rendition when great Auntie Betty comes to visit.

My dad

[to the tune of 'My Bonnie Lies Over the Ocean']
My dad is a lavatory cleaner
He works all the day and the night
And when he comes home in the morning
His boots are all covered in
Shine up your buttons with Brasso
It's only five pennies a tin

You can nick it from Woolies if you want to
As long as there's nobody in

Some say that he died of a fever
Some say that he died of a fright
But I know what my old dad died of
He died of the smell of the

Shine up your buttons ...

Mary had a little lamb

[you will never be able to repeat the clean version after this]
Mary had a little lamb
She thought it rather silly
So she threw it up into the air
And caught it by its

Willy was a sheepdog
Lying in the grass
Along came a mosquito
And bit it on the

Ask no questions
Tell no lies
Have you ever seen a postman
Doing up his

Flies are awful
Bees are worse
And that is the end
Of this silly little verse!

Fairy story crib sheet

If you can't remember all the words to lullabies, then at least people can get together the basics of most well-known fairy stories. Or can they? What happens once Red Riding Hood discovers that grandma is a big, bad wolf? What did the bears do to Goldilocks when they found her asleep in bed. Here are the crib notes versions of classic bedtime stories.

Little Red Riding Hood

A little girl in a red coat meets a wolf when she's on her way to Granny's house with some goodies. Wolf fancies a supper of little girl so beats her to the house, tricking Granny to let him in. He eats Granny and puts on her clothes. Red Riding Hood is surprised how big Granny's eyes and teeth look, and gets gobbled up too. Her dad happens to be passing and hears Granny snoring. He sees the wolf in Granny's bed but thinks that maybe he's eaten her. So he cuts the wolf open and finds Granny and Red Riding Hood, both alive. He fills the wolf's stomach with stones and it can't get up and chase them and dies. Everyone lives happily ever after.

Goldilocks

A girl comes across a house belonging to a family of three bears – Mummy bear, Daddy bear and Baby bear. They've popped out and left their porridge cooling so naturally the girl decides to snaffle some. Dad's is too hot, Mum's too sweet Baby's is just right. Then she sits down but Dad's chair is too big, Mum's too squashy and Baby's just right – but she breaks it. So, instead, she wants a lie down and goes upstairs to bed. Dad's is too hard, Mum's is too soft but Baby's is just right. The bears come back, each exclaiming that someone's been at their porridge/chair/bed until Baby discovers Goldilocks still in bed. They frighten her awake and she runs away. The end.

Rapunzel

A man and his wife really wanted to pinch the veg in their neighbour's garden, but she was a witch. They gave into temptation and the witch caught them. She was going to kill them but instead demanded their first born. She took the girl and locked her up in a tall tower with no door or stairs. If she wanted to get in, the girl – Rapunzel – had to dangle her hair out of the window so the witch could climb up. One day, a prince climbed up instead because he liked her singing and they hatched a plan so she could escape. But the silly girl put her foot in it and asked the witch why she was heavier than the prince. The witch was miffed that someone else was able to see her, so cut off her hair and sent Rapunzel into exile. She tricked the prince with Rapunzel's hair, so he jumped out of the tower to escape but fell down and was blinded. He roamed around for years until he heard her singing again and she cried when she saw him, which cured his blindness. Everyone lived happily ever after.

Rumpelstiltskin

A really stupid man tells the king that his really pretty daughter can make gold from straw so the king locks her in a dungeon and says, 'If this room isn't full of gold tomorrow I'll kill you.' She's a bit upset by this until a little man appears and does the job for her, as long as she gives him her jewellery. The king is really impressed and says if she manages to do one more big job, he'll marry her. She can't pay the little man any more but he says he'll accept her first-born in exchange. Off she goes and marries the king and has a child and, understandably, doesn't really want to hand him over. The little man says he'll let her off if she can find out his name. She sends out a spy who finds him dancing round a fire calling, 'Rumplestiltskin.' The queen tells him she knows his name and he gets so miffed that he tears himself into bits. Everyone (else) lives happily ever after.

The frog king

The king has a really, really pretty daughter but she's a bit daft because the silly girl drops her favourite toy down a well. An ugly frog rescues it, on condition it can live with her and be her bestest friend. She agrees but when she gets her toy back, reneges on the deal and runs back to Daddy. The frog eventually makes it to the castle, but the princess slams the door in its face. The king says a promise is a promise and makes her eat, sleep and play with the frog. The princess is more than a little bit peeved and chucks the frog against the wall. Frog turns into handsome, kind king who insists on taking her to his fabulous kingdom where they live happily ever after.

The princess and the pea

Girl turns up at an eligible prince's castle in a storm looking like a drowned rat but insisting she's a princess. Potential future mother-in-law isn't convinced so puts a hard pea in the girl's bed, sticks 20 mattresses on top and sends her to bed. Girl gets up next morning and complains of the most uncomfortable night's sleep, which convinces the mother-in-law that she's the real deal because only a princess could be that sensitive. Everyone gets married and lives happily ever after.

There are two morals here: one, princesses are stuck-up little madams who are never happy. Two, mother-in-laws will never believe that you are good enough for their sons, even if you are a princess.

Chapter Eleven

Some strange stuff

'Why?' ... 'Because.'

Mum's default response to any question. Usually employed when you've been put on the spot, have too many other things to think about and it's the only answer you can think of. This, or its slightly less satisfying cousin: 'It just is.'

It was precisely for this reason that old wives' tales were invented. Clearly so-called because old wives were mums, and mums know everything and need to be seen to know everything. And, therefore, for everything that you don't instantly have a true or even plausible answer for, there is an old wives' tale.

Some tales are based on long-forgotten fact and folklore. Some even have a fairly decent rationale behind them. Most are just completely bonkers.

Carrots make you see in the dark

While the vitamins in carrots are beneficial for eyesight, there's nowhere near enough in a portion to have any impact. Instead, this was a myth spread on purpose by the British Army in the Second World War. The rumour was that airmen were eating lots of carrots and that's what gave them an uncanny ability to hit German targets in the dead of night. What they were in fact doing was trying to cover up the development of their fab new toy: Radar.

If you were to try this theory out, you could indeed eat lots of carrots. However, you would go orange from another essential vitamin, betacarotene, before you could see any better. This is absolutely true.

Chocolate gives you spots

There's no conclusive evidence that it does, but a bad diet in general won't contribute to a glowing complexion. Acne is usually a result of hormonal changes during puberty, oily make-up and, bizarrely, washing your face too much. Some medicine can also create breakouts. Stress can make them worse, but won't cause them in the first place so it's still not a medical reason to avoid your exams.

Dandelions make you wet the bed

The thought that dandelions cause bed-wetting is down to their folkloric names, in English, 'pissabed', and in French, '*pissenlit*'. While dandelion extract is a natural diuretic, you would have to be eating them to get the effect. Just looking at, smelling or even blowing the dandelion clocks has no effect.

The eternal chewing gum

If you swallow your chewing gum, it will stay in your tummy for ever. If you keep swallowing it, it will build up until there's no room for anything else and you'll *die*! Actually, that's not true as anything that can't be digested, like gum and All Bran, is passed straight through the body.

Hairy tales

A variety of healthy foods are supposed to alternately make your hair curly (bread crusts), make your hair shine (raw eggs, fish oil) or put hairs on your chest (meat, chillies). While, as part of a balanced diet, they might

contribute to the overall condition of your hair, they don't have these specific, immediate abilities.

Going outside with wet hair and no coat makes you ill

The sight of an underdressed youth heading into the chilly air used to cause our grandmothers to shriek, 'You'll catch your death!', inferring that exposure to the cold caused, at best, sniffles, and, at worst, fully fledged pneumonia. Neither the common cold, nor 'flu, nor pneumonia can be caused by just getting cold. They're all the result of viruses or bugs. Although recent research does suggest that getting cold makes you more vulnerable to catching colds.

Square eyes

To try to prise me away from the box, my parents would try to convince me I'd get square eyes. As deterrents go, it was pretty ineffective, and also untrue. Sitting too close to the television and watching it for long periods at a time will inevitably damage your eyesight, although it is impossible to change the shape to square.

Funny face

'If you pull that face and the wind changes, you'll stay like that ...' No, you won't, but somehow kids believe it. Don't question it, it works.

Monday's child

If you're willing to accept that the month you're born in has some kind of bearing on your personality (Libra – wimp, Cancer – shifty, Scorpio – nasty) then you'll happily believe that the day you were born on influences you too.

The old nursery rhyme goes:

Monday's child is fair of face
Tuesday's child is full of grace
Wednesday's child is full of woe
Thursday's child has far to go
Friday's child is loving and giving
Saturday's child works hard for a living
But the child who is born on the Sabbath Day
Is fair and wise and good and gay

Bless you

This was originally 'God Bless You', said after someone sneezed. Some think this originates during the time of the Black Death, when the bubonic plague ravaged Europe. In fact, the disease's main symptom wasn't sneezing, but enormous pus-filled blisters. However, many at the time believed the disease was spread by sneezing, and people used to believe it was the origin of the playground rhyme, 'Ring a Ring o' Roses'

Ring a ring o' Roses

*[a ring of flowers was supposed to ward off noxious humours, or
    smells]*

A pocket full of posies

*[a collection of medicinal herbs was kept about the body of healthy
    people to ward off the disease]*

Atishoo, Atishoo

*[the sneezing that was supposed to accompany the illness – but
    didn't]*

We all fall down

[dead]

The fact that the song doesn't mention exploding pustules of yellow,
disease-ridden fluid makes the likelihood that the song is in fact linked to
the plague unrealistic. Good gory story, though, and a way to encourage
the young 'uns to cover their mouths when they sneeze.

Chocolate gives dogs worms

In a bid to discourage kids from giving pets treats under the table, parents
would say that the dog would get worms. Actually, you're better off going
for the truth in this case, it makes a much bigger impact: chocolate kills
dogs.

Chocs made for human consumption contain a compound called
theobromine. It does nothing bad to people but can be very toxic for
animals, including dogs. One chocolate button isn't something to worry
about but more, particularly on a small dog, can be fatal.

If your kids are intent on spoiling Fido, you can get 'dog drops' from
the pet store or supermarket, which look a bit chocolatey. As for kids
eating dog chocolate? That's fine but *eugh!*, it tastes *awful*!

Superstitions

Superstitions are much like old wives' tales or urban myths, but just tend to be that one degree loopier.

Butter side down

Allowing bread to fall butter side down was considered to be a sign that bad luck was on its way. Personally, I think it's bad luck because you get butter on the carpet and fluff in your sandwich.

Break empty eggshells

Once you've had your runny egg and soldiers, you should push your spoon through the bottom of the shell. In the time of Henry VIII, it was believed that witches could take shells that were complete apart from their tops and make boats to sink ships.

They couldn't actually fit inside the shells and sail them. Instead, they were thought to do some kind of voodoo by floating the shells in some water and then shaking up the water to simulate a storm, in which the real boat would then be wrecked.

Spilling salt

Salt is linked to crying (just try getting some in your eye) so spilling it represents tears, and, therefore, bad luck. However, you can counteract some of this bad luck if you take a pinch of the spilt salt and throw it over your left shoulder. It's supposed to hit the devil and knock him off your shoulder. Most likely though, spilling salt was bad luck because historically it was expensive and you'd be quite literally chucking money away.

Gold at the end of the rainbow

Myth: It's commonly thought that leprechauns, little Irish fairies with

magical powers, would hide their stash of gold at the end of the rainbow. It's actually a trick that a leprechaun played on a poor couple. He'd offered to help them when he heard their plight, but he was offended when they asked for gold to buy nice things, instead of basics like food and clothing. So he told them that the gold was hidden at the end of the rainbow, and they've been searching for it ever since. You'll know that if you've ever tried to catch up with a rainbow it's impossible.

Lightning never strikes twice

Rubbish. And I don't intend to stand out in a storm hanging onto a long bit of metal to test the theory.

Unlucky numbers

I consider any number that doesn't come up on my Lottery ticket to be unlucky, but there are two in particular that give people the heebie-jeebies …

666

Considered to be the devil's number. Some think it's just a handy inversion of 999, the number to call for the emergency services in the UK. It goes back to the Bible, in the book of Revelations ch13, v16–18, which ascribes a number to the devil as a way to identify him:

'He causes all, both small and great, rich and poor, free and slave, to receive a mark on their right hand or on their foreheads,
and that no one may buy or sell except one who has the mark or the name of the beast, or the number of his name.
Here is wisdom. Let him who has understanding calculate the number of the beast, for it is the number of a man: His number is 666.'

13

This number is usually prefixed by the word 'unlucky', in case you were in any doubt. This is allegedly because there were 13 people at the Last Supper, the event at which Jesus revealed he had been betrayed. Such is the power of this number that whole streets and tower blocks are built without house number 13 or a 13th floor.

Traditionally, people also try to avoid doing anything of consequence on Friday 13th, which is considered to be doubly unlucky (Jesus was crucified on a Friday).

Some people really do get very disturbed by the portents brought by the number 13, and avoid it at all costs. Show what a smart arse you are by calling them triskaideckophobes – having a phobia of the number 13 – and pick up a world-beating Scrabble score into the bargain.

Walking under a ladder

There are several possible reasons why it was considered unlucky to walk under a ladder. For one, it represents the ladder up to the gallows, and a date with the hangman. Another interpretation is that the wall, the ladder and the pavement form a triangle representing the three sides of the Holy Trinity: Father, Son and Holy Ghost. To walk through the middle of this is to disrespect the Trinity.

An altogether more credible alternative is that walking under the ladder puts you at very real risk of getting hit on the head by a 10-litre tin of vinyl gloss paint, or whatever else the bloke at the top had in his hands when his mobile rang.

Cracks in the pavement

While many kids, and some adults, will skip along the pavements trying to avoid the cracks, few know that this superstition has some pretty unpleasant roots. In the 1800s, when racism wasn't just accepted but expected, it was suggested that if you stood on the cracks you would have a black baby, or your mother would turn black – inferring that black was not a positive colour to be. Fortunately, times change and, since the 1950s, the rhyme that accompanies skipping over the cracks goes: *'Step on a crack, break your mother's back.'*

Lighting three cigarettes with the same match

While I sincerely hope your kids don't take up the dreaded weed, the story's still a good one. You might want to translate the myth to lighting a candle or a barbeque to make it more suitable for young ears.

Despite the temptation to eke out scarce resources, soldiers in the trenches in the First World War were instructed never to share the light from one match – their very lives depended on it. Lighting the first cigarette alerted the Germans to the soldiers' position. Passing it to the second gave the sniper time to load his gun. Passing it to the third gave him time to fire. The associated bad luck stays to this day.

Touch wood

Used like a 'get out of jail free' card, saying 'touch wood' takes the bad luck out of talking about an unwanted event, and protects the speaker against it coming true. For the serious-minded, it has its origins in the protection offered by the wooden crucifix. The less religious think it's simply an extension of the childhood game, tag, where players were safe from tagging if they were touching something wooden, like a tree.

Pointing

We spend much of our kids younger years teaching them what things are by pointing at them. Then we go and confuse the poor wee mites by telling them it's rude to point. But why?

It was thought that all the evil in a person was held in the index finger (have you tried pointing with your pinky?), and by pointing it at someone you were cursing them with that evil. Pointing at a funeral procession was even worse, as it was thought you'd bring another death to the town.

Coins in the fountain

If you throw a coin in a fountain while making a wish it's supposed to come true. However, if you happened to have bits of human sacrifice hanging around, it's a good idea to lob them in too. The water is supposed to hold all manner of gods and spirits that, if legend is to be believed, are in a permanently bad mood. Only a tasty bit of pancreas will lift the gloom. With that in mind, 10p seems like a small price to pay …

Shoes and hats on the table

The table was considered to be the altar at the centre of the household, and to put outdoor items, such as hats and shoes, on it was disrespectful. The lore then grew up that to do so would bring a death to the family.

A more practical explanation is that neither item is hygienic to have in close contact with food and where people eat.

Leaving shoes and hats on beds is just as bad. In this case, the hat was symbolic of a death because if a doctor rushed to someone's sick bed, they'd have no time to lose and kept their hat on while they worked. If they arrived and put their hat on the bed, it showed that the patient was beyond any help.

Opening an umbrella indoors

There seems to be no strong background to why this has become widespread, other than the fact that it looks strange. Practicality might have a simple answer – a brolly of any size will play havoc with trinkets on mantelpieces, books on bookshelves and the eyes and ears of anyone unfortunate to be in close proximity.

Turning the calendar over prematurely

A symbol of the other well-known phrase 'tempting fate'. To turn the page before the date was to assume that you would be alive and well to perform whatever duties you had planned, when any fool knows your fate is not in your hands. It brings to mind a well-worn joke: 'How do you make God laugh? ... Tell him your plans.'

Black cats

Thought to have its origins in Ancient Egypt where the cat was a god: Bast, daughter of Ra, the sun god. Thus, all black cats were thought to have supernatural powers, which were generally viewed by the superstitious several hundred years ago as being 'A Bad Thing'.

That view changed over time, and now meeting a black cat is thought to bring good luck – but only if it's walking towards you. If it crosses your path, we're back to bad luck again. Some miners and fishermen would turn on their heels and go back home again if one crossed their path in the morning on their way to work.

Magpies

Magpies are infamous for pinching pretty, shiny things to decorate their nest but, like many superstitions, have the roots of their bad reputation in religion. It is thought that its distinctive black-and-white colouring made it the bastard child of a dove and a raven (how symbolic do you want to get?) and because it was born out of wedlock (how do birds of different species get married again?), it wasn't baptised like the rest of God's creatures.

It was considered to counteract your bad luck by greeting magpies in the customary fashion:

> 'Morning/Afternoon, Mr Magpie. How's Mrs Magpie and all the
> little Magpies?'

There's also a counting rhyme that tells you the consequences depending on how many magpies you see at one time:

One for sorrow, two for mirth,
Three for a wedding, four for a birth,
Five for silver, six for gold,
Seven for a secret not to be told.
Eight for heaven, nine for hell,
And ten for the devil's own sel'.

Ravens in the Tower

Ravens don't get an entirely bad press, however. They protect one of the UK's most recognisable landmarks, the Tower of London, and some say even the monarchy itself.

Nobody knows when ravens first came to the Tower of London, but they've been associated with it for centuries. Legend dictates that, if the ravens ever leave, the Tower will fall and the Kingdom will fall, so Charles II decreed that there must always be at least six ravens at the Tower. That tradition has been honoured for more than 300 years. To keep the birds from flying away, the Raven Master clips their lifting feathers. The procedure doesn't hurt them in any way; it simply unbalances their flight so they won't stray from the Tower.

Peacock feather

Some people believe the pattern on a peacock feather resembles the evil eye. Because of this, they believe it can spy on the household, which generally brings bad luck. Some believe that bringing it into the house of an unmarried woman forces her to stay a spinster for ever. Actors also avoid them, believing they doom their performance. There are few people more superstitious than actors.

Killing a spider

It's generally bad luck to kill a spider, particularly of the money sort. Cobwebs are also supposed to have mystical powers, including the ability to bandage wounds. I hope you've got a strong stomach for the next bit: Apparently, carrying a decomposing spider around in a bag round your neck is supposed to cure disease.

Things my mother taught me

My mother taught me RELIGION:
'You better pray that will come out of the carpet.'

My mother taught me about TIME TRAVEL:
'If you don't straighten up, I'm going to knock you into the middle of
next week!'

My mother taught me LOGIC:
'If you fall out of that swing and break your neck, you're not going
to the shops with me.'

My mother taught me about the science of OSMOSIS:
'Shut your mouth and eat your supper!'

My mother taught me about ANTICIPATION:
'Just wait until we get home.'

And my all-time favorite …

My mother taught me about JUSTICE:
'One day you'll have kids … and I hope they turn out just like you!'

Chapter Twelve

Some sore stuff

Mums are the default setting when it comes to kids toppling over and breaking themselves. We're also expected to perform miracles for dads who are fully convinced they're about to die from a bout of man-flu. Many day-to-day accidents and illnesses can be improved by the judicious application of cuddles, kisses and some medicinal chocolate. But, occasionally, you might actually have to do something medical to make your children better.

I'm going to deal with fairly basic, minor bumps and illnesses that you can treat at home. There are lots of manuals to teach you how to do CPR (cardiopulmonary resuscitation) and what to do if small children take a pair of scissors to the extension cable, and it's better to use those than take advice from a make do and mender like me. My advice is: if it scares you, scares Dad and scares the kids, call the doc and scare them too.

Common cold

Unfortunately, you can catch a cold from anyone, and anything. Poor hygiene is often the reason that it goes round a whole family like a dose of salts. Everyone knows they should cover their mouth and nose when they sneeze and cough, but you can also pick up a cold from using the same doorhandle, cup etc. If you're around someone who's streaming, get them to wash their hands, and make sure you wash yours frequently too.

We all know that there is no cure for the common cold but there are remedies that can make it a bit more bearable. Many of these can be bought over the counter but you can make some out of what's knocking around in the kitchen cupboard.

Sore throat: Get a teaspoonful of butter and roll it in sugar. Place it near the back of the tongue and let it gently melt down the throat. Sounds foul, but my granny swore by it and I had butter and sugar shoved down my throat for years.

Blocked nose: You need oil of eucalyptus, a big bowl of very hot water and a towel. The old remedy of putting drops of a decongestant oil such as eucalyptus in a bowl of water, then inhaling the steam is remarkably comforting and a lot cheaper than commercial inhalers that have much the same effect.

General cruddy feeling: Vitamin C is supposed to be a great defence against the cold, and though it's a bit like shutting the stable door after the horse has bolted, it can't hurt to stock up on a few vits. Squeeze a lemon into some hot water and add in a goodly dollop of honey. Stir well and sip. Of course, this is the child-friendly version.

If you yourself are suffering, make a hot toddy by adding a very generous slug of whisky or brandy once the water has cooled a bit.

But if we're being sensible, there's also hot milk and honey, which can be poshed up with a bit of froth and topped with ground nutmeg or cinnamon. The medicinal properties of this are debatable but it aids sleep and provides nutrition if you've lost your appetite, or are having difficulty swallowing.

Feed a cold, starve a fever: This old-wives' tale is nonsense. In fact, with a fever, you are likely to need even more food as your body is burning more calories. The best advice is to keep trying to eat normal amounts of nutritious food and drink plenty of fluids in both cases. Chicken soup is the famous remedy, with plenty of protein from the meat, vitamins from the veg and warm liquids. Making it garlicky is also a good plan as it's supposed to ward off diseases, as well as vampires.

Is it a cold or flu: A doctor will be able to determine this with a simple test, but you could use your own yardstick. If a tenner was stapled to the outside of your door, would you get out of bed to go and get it? If you said, 'Yes,' you have a cold. If you sneeze in disgust and go back to sleep then it may be flu. For the younger generation, replace the ten-pound note with a Playstation game.

Insect stings

Bees leave the sting behind, wasps don't. You have the gratifying knowledge that the bee paid for your pain with its life. Unfortunately, the wasp goes on to sting another day.

If someone is unfortunate enough to get stung and the sting is still there, you'll need a pair of sharp-ended tweezers to get it out. It's the only thing in wasps' favour that they don't leave the sting behind, because it means you only get one quick dose of the poison. The bee leaves the sting behind with its poison sac attached so you have to be careful removing it. The sac if left or squeezed by the tweezers will continue pumping poison into the injury, which can get quite painful after a while. So it's important when removing the sting to get the tweezers as close to the skin as possible to get below the sac.

There are lots of anti-sting creams to reduce the redness and pain of a sting, but a cold compress – a cold, wet flannel for example – will do the job just as well. Leave the compress on the sting area for about 10 minutes, or until the pain has gone.

Because wasps often go for the sweet stuff, it has been known for them to get inside cans of soft drinks and then sting inside the mouth. Decant cans into glasses during the wasp season. Having a cold drink or sucking an ice cube will help to soothe the sting but the casualty should also see a doctor.

Jellyfish stings

The sting of the jellyfish is in those pretty tentacles that dangle off its half-moon shaped body. All jellyfish have them, but some are worse than others. The most notorious is the Portuguese man-of-war, which packs a punch. The most common in the UK is the moon jellyfish, which is more of an irritation. Contrary to popular belief, they can still sting when they're all washed up and dead on the shoreline, so prodding it with your big toe isn't the cleverest idea.

One recognised remedy is to pour vinegar over the sting and then dust with meat tenderiser. Personally, I don't take either of those to the beach, but there is another remedy that does the trick. That's right, wee on it! Now for everyone that says this works, another will say it doesn't, and another will say that it makes the sting worse.

Insect and jellyfish stings can be a cause of anaphylactic shock.

Anaphylactic shock is a severe allergic reaction to stings, bites, medicines or foods such as peanuts. Sometimes you are already aware of the things that you might be allergic to, and can take steps to avoid them. Others catch you unawares.

The symptoms of anaphylactic shock range from:
- Anxiety
- Red, blotchy skin
- Swelling of face, neck and tongue
- Puffiness around the eyes
- Wheezing
- Difficulty breathing
- Rapid pulse

In every case where you suspect anaphylactic shock, call an ambulance and tell the controller this is what you think might be wrong, and, if possible, what may have triggered it. They can make sure the ambulance crew has the correct medication to reverse it.

While waiting for an ambulance, help the casualty to breathe by propping up their torso. Don't lie them flat on the ground. If they lose consciousness put them in the recovery position. Loosen any tight clothing, particularly around the neck, chest and waist.

While an attack can come on very rapidly, within a few minutes of the trigger happening, the medicines developed to counter it also take effect almost immediately.

Splinters

It's amazing how such a tiny little bit of nothing can cause you to writhe in agony. That agony is only compounded by the sight of Mum looming on the horizon with a pair of tweezers threatening to take it out. Often if it was left, a small splinter would just be absorbed by the body and vanish without trace. However, it could be from somewhere particularly dirty, or encourage a secondary infection so, as the saying goes, better out than in!

Wash the area with soap and warm water. Make sure your tweezers are clean and sterile. You can sterilise metal by holding it in a flame for a few seconds. Remember to let it cool before attacking the offending article or you'll have even more howling to deal with. If the ends of the tweezers go black with soot, don't be tempted to wipe it off. Even though it looks dirty, it's still cleaner than the ends of your fingers.

Hold the bit of person that the splinter is in gently but firmly, and with the tweezers in the other hand get as close to the skin as possible. By grabbing the splinter at its tip, you'll just pull the end off, making it harder to pull out cleanly.

Pull the splinter out as close as possible to the angle it went in at. Once you're sure that the whole thing is out, squeeze the injured part (I know, this all sounds like an exercise in sadism) to get a little bit of blood. That should carry with it any dirt that was embedded with the splinter. Wash again, pat dry, and stick a plaster on.

Nosebleeds

I used to love nosebleeds because they are thoroughly dramatic while being pretty much painless. Of course, if they've been caused by a 'head meets hard object' incident, the last bit isn't strictly true, but mine tended to be quite random and impressive.

They're simple to treat. Sit down with the head tilted quite far forward. Pinch the soft bit of the nose (i.e. below the bridge) together and breathe through the mouth. Stay like this for about 10 minutes. When the gushing's stopped, clean up gently and try to avoid sneezing, blowing noses or indeed any form of digital exploration for at least a few hours. If it goes on for longer than about half an hour, there's lots and lots of blood or it happens again and again, see a doctor.

Typical first-aid kit

If I were the organised Girl Guide sort of person, I would have a fully stocked and inventoried first-aid kit in my house. What I actually have is a couple of old plasters, some ibuprofen and a lot of bog roll. These do the trick at a pinch, but they're not ideal.

A basic first-aid kit contains:

- Small scissors
- Sharp ended tweezers
- Antiseptic/local anaesthetic cream
- Sterile non-adhesive pad
- Plasters – various sizes
- Gauze swabs
- Sterile dressing – at least two
- Bandage – various sizes
- Hypoallergenic tape

Blisters

No one escapes blisters. I bet even the Queen gets walkabout blisters and has a special blister-flunky to deal with them. The important thing with blisters is not to do what everyone does. Fiddle, poke and play with them until they burst. Yes, it's very satisfying but no, it's not a good idea. You've now got an open wound that can get infected.

Instead of popping it, wash it with soap and water, dry and cover with a plaster. Boring isn't it? An ordinary plaster will do (make sure the cushioned pad more than covers the blister) but you can buy fancy new jelly ones that claim they suck the blister dry causing it to drop off when it's healed.

Cuts and grazes

How is it that you can hear people on the news say that they walked almost all the way home before realising they'd been shot, and yet a grazed knee feels like your leg is dropping off. And often, the treatment is worse than the accident. At least for gunshot wounds, the hospital gives you lots of lovely drugs. For a graze the best you can expect is a lollypop and a hankie.

Wash the graze gently with soap (*ow!*) and water using a gauze pad, or some soft tissue paper. Try to brush out any bits of stones or playground still lurking in the wound, which may make it bleed even more (*oww!*). Press a clean, dry pad of gauze or tissue on the wound to stop any more bleeding and dry off the area. Cover with a breathable plaster.

Hiccups

Drinking backwards from a cup of water, holding your breath and trying to scare someone are all time-honoured ways of trying to stop hiccups. I've had limited success with all of them but backwards water seems to work best. Eventually, they will go away of their own accord if you do nothing, but it is worthwhile having a bash at stopping them because if hiccups go on for a long time it can be painful on the chest and exhausting.

To drink backwards, put water in a wide-mouthed cup. Tip your head forward and put your mouth over the far side of the cup. Then tip the cup away from you so that the water goes in under your top lip. Pour enough so you can get a drink (gulping fresh air is just going to make the hiccups worse). I don't think this method works scientifically, but you spend so long figuring out how to do it without spilling water up your nose that it takes your mind off the hiccups, thus curing you.

Cut mouth

Put a pad over the wound and put pressure on the cut for 10 minutes. Don't wash the mouth out because you want the blood to clot to stem the bleeding.

Sometimes the mouth injury is a tooth that's gone flying. If it's a baby tooth then at least it will grow back, but adult teeth don't. If you manage to find the tooth (always a good idea to look for it in case it's been swallowed), put it in milk as a good dentist may be able to 'replant' it. (The milk keeps bacteria out and the blood vessels alive!)

The hole where the tooth was will undoubtedly be bleeding, so put a pad of tissue or cotton wool firmly in the space. Make it a big lump so that it can be bitten down on. The pressure should stop the bleeding. Next stop, dentist for a new gnasher.

Burns and scalds

Rinse the affected area under cold water as soon as possible and for at least 10 minutes. Not only does it relieve the pain, but it also stops the skin 'cooking' as the burn continues to do damage even once the heat source has been removed.

Only try to take clothing off the burned area when the burn has cooled. Cover the burn with non-fluffy cloth such as a pillowcase. Cover burnt limbs with plastic bags or cling film. Burns will blister and severe burns have open sores almost immediately so should be covered to prevent infection. All severe burns should be seen by a doctor. The treatment is the same for chemical burns, but the symptoms of these take longer to show up.

Eye injuries

Just looking at someone with a sore eye makes your eyes water in sympathy. But, you only get one set of eyes so you need to take care of them.

'Something' in the eye: Tip the casualty's head back and hold the eyelids open. Get them to look up, down, left and right to help you see what's stuck in there. If you can see it, try slowly pouring a jug of water over the eye, starting at the inside corner so the water washes over the whole of the eye. If that doesn't work, try using a damp handkerchief to gently brush it out or lift it off. If something is stuck under the eyelid, try lifting the top eyelid over the lower to move it out. If the object looks as if it's actually stuck in, not just lying on top of, the eye, hold a wad of tissue over the affected eye and get thee to casualty. This isn't a DIY job.

Chemicals: Holding the head under cold running water, sluice any chemicals out for at least 10 minutes. If only one eye is affected, keep the good eye at the top, out of the way of the water. If you prefer, you can ask the casualty lie on the floor and use a jug of water instead. Cover the eye with a pad and seek medical advice.

Swallowing things

Kids of any age are forever putting things in their mouths that they're not supposed to, and rarely put anything in that they are (i.e. vegetables).

If your child seems to have swallowed something, try to get hold of an example of it. Then if you can't identify it, a professional can. Don't try to make them sick, it only makes things worse. If there are still bits of the thing they've swallowed in their mouth, try to hook them out. Be very careful and don't prod hard or scrape the back of the throat. Also, don't try to use another implement to extract the object. If they've swallowed chemicals, give small sips of milk as their lips and mouth may well be burned.

If they've inhaled something instead, they're likely be coughing hard. Tip them over your knee so the head is lower than their torso (as if you were about to give them a good spanking – not that you would) Make sharp, hard slaps between the shoulder blades to dislodge the object.

Bumps on the head

Usually, a bump on the head is accompanied by a nice egg right in the middle of the forehead and a comment from some old bloke: 'That'll knock some sense into them.'

However, there are times when they crack themselves a good 'un. In case of concussion, apply a cold compress to the head and sit quietly with them for a while. With slight concussion they will probably lose consciousness briefly (less than 20 seconds), feel a bit sick on coming round, be a bit dizzy and have little memory of what just happened. After 30 minutes, they should have nothing more than a slight headache. If they're still poorly or not quite themselves after that time, call a doctor.

Sprained ankle

If the casualty can't take their full weight on the affected limb it's probably a sprain. If they can't take any weight at all, it looks like it's swelling up really quite impressively (a little swelling with a sprain is to be expected) and there's lots of yowling then it could be a break. A twisted ankle on the other hand hurts for a few minutes, but after a little hobbling pretty much rights itself.

With a sprain, take shoes and socks off before the swelling makes this too tricky. Get the casualty to sit with their leg raised and put a cold compress on to minimise the swelling. Bandage firmly, with cotton-wool padding if possible, round the ankle and foot. But not so firmly that you cut off all circulation!

Trapped fingers

Run the fingers under a cold tap until the pain goes away. If the swelling doesn't go down, the fingers still can't be moved after a while, the fingers may have been broken, so seek medical advice.

Sunburn

Slip, slap, slop – that's what our Aussie cousins are always telling us, and do we pay any attention? What, when we have 3½ days of sunshine a year and skin that's a light shade of cornflower blue? Not a chance.

So naturally being both unused to and obsessed with the sun, we dash out into it half naked the first chance we get. Then we dash back inside again two hours later the colour of a well-done lobster.

We've all got our lobster stories but the simple fact is you should do everything you can to avoid getting sunburn, particularly children on whom it's been proven to hasten the potential onset of skin cancer. But we're not perfect and even a cloudy day can be deceptive so what do you do if you end up glowing gently in the dark? There's not a lot you can do other than move inside, take lots of cool fluids and apply after sun cream or calamine lotion, which can take the heat and the sting out of the burnt skin.

If you've been out in the sun and start feeling dizzy and headachey with a rapid pulse it's possible that you've got heatstroke. In this case, take off all outer clothing, lie the patient down in a cool, darkened room, sponge down with cool water and a flannel and fan if possible. It's always best to call a doctor for a check up.

Fever

When kids hold their hands to their heads, look all wobbly and say they feel hot, check the following:

- Is it a school day?
- Is it games?
- Is there a test?
- Are they chancers?

A genuine temperature, or fever, is anything above 37°C. A degree and a bit over isn't a great concern, but anything above 40°C can be dangerous.

The hand on the forehead trick isn't a very accurate way of determining if someone has a fever. You do need to use a thermometer. Small children don't readily cooperate using the mouth method, so the best place to take a temperature is under the armpit. Fold the arm back down so the thermometer is nice and snug while you're taking the reading. The time needed varies according to type of thermometer so read the instructions.

If a fever is present, the patient won't just have a high temperature, but could also be quite pale, and despite being hot, they'll be chittering or complaining of feeling cold.

Let the patient lie down but don't swaddle them in bedclothes, even if they complain of being cold. GPs moan that well-meaning parents have virtually cooked their children by wrapping them up in layers of blankets. Give plenty of fluids and some infant paracetamol which can help bring down a fever. If they're very very hot, you might want to sponge them with tepid water and let it dry in the air, which helps to cool the skin.

Fever can be a sign of meningitis

Meningitis is a terrifying illness for any parent but we fortunately know so much more about how to diagnose and treat it now.

Symptoms include some, but not all, of:

- Fever
- Listlessness
- Vomiting
- Loss of appetite
- Headache
- Sensitivity to light
- Cold extremities (hands and feet)
- Stiff neck
- Purple rash that doesn't disappear when pressed with a glass
- Sudden change for the worse

Many of these symptoms occur in ordinary childhood illnesses, which is hardly reassuring when you're trying to make a diagnosis. Parents who have experienced children with meningitis explain that while they'd seen many of the symptoms before, there was just something about the way their child looked and behaved that was very out of the ordinary. Hardly scientific but reassuring that the instinct you have that something isn't quite right is what you should pay attention to.

The best way to act with meningitis is quickly, so if you suspect something and it turns out to be nothing, that's a far better outcome than the other way round. Call the doctor, and if you don't feel the response is going to be quick enough, go straight to Accident and Emergency.

Tummy-aches and vomiting

There's not a lot you can do with vomiting, except let it run its course and get busy with lots of kitchen towel and disinfectant. Give plenty of fluids, even if you think they'll come up again, because they'll keep the patient hydrated and give them a chance to get the nasty taste out of their mouth. Always keep a trusty bowl handy.

A tummy-ache may not necessarily lead to vomiting, but keep a bowl handy anyway. Sometimes a hot water bottle can ease any pain. Don't try to get the patient to eat.

Earache

Even if it feels like it's usually the kids giving you earache, sometimes they suffer from the genuine article. Lying flat can often make the symptoms worse, so put the patient to bed propped up on pillows. Give the recommended dose of infant paracetamol and get out the trusty hot water bottle. You don't want it too hot, but encourage them to lie with the affected side of the head against the bottle.

Toothache

A pain in your teeth is one of the worst imaginable, which is why filmmakers used it to great effect in the torture scene in *Marathon Man*. Apart from the unavoidable appointment with the dentist, all you can do is give infant paracetamol and hope that does the trick. If the pain is along the gumline, you can try rubbing oil of cloves on a fingertip along the gums which can have a remarkably soothing effect, but it's temporary and boy does it stink!

Throwing a sickie

Everyone's thrown a sickie once. Perhaps there was a test, or a cross-country 10K run planned in the pouring rain. I don't know anyone whose main goal in life was to acquire a 100% school attendance record. I don't know many who are trying to achieve it at work either.

But, once you get to be a mum – that is, a grown-up – the tables are turned and you get to bust the sickie-takers. And it's not as easy as it sounds. Unless you're a bona fide doctor, it's hard to tell if that dizzy sick feeling is a result of the undercooked sausages you served up last night, or double biology later this morning. The last thing you want is to be called to Matron's office in school to pick up an obviously ill child from a tutting Hattie Jacques lookalike.

But you don't want to look like a mug. Here are some of the tricks kids use to get a free duvet day. It's a case of know thine enemy (and who knows, they might just sound convincing down the phone to your boss too.)

Sickness of choice

Most malingerers will go for a suitably vague, non-chronic complaint, such as stomach-ache, 24-hour bug, headache or diarrhoea. Handy for them because the most extensive examination revolves around how generally off-colour they look and the most invasive treatment is an aspirin and a bottle of Lucozade.

More practised sickie-takers will start to hint at oncoming symptoms the night before. Real pros will start to complain when they get back from school the previous day, but will troop off and finish their homework like good little soldiers, before making a feeble attempt at the night's dinner. Thus, the scene is set for genuine concern the next morning.

Even more complex is the multi-friend sickie set-up, where whole groups of friends arrange to be sick in sequence. As one 'recovers' from a stomach bug, the next one goes down with it and so on. It takes a bit of detective work and some calling around to uncover the truth of this one.

Novices however, hope to go from perfect to poorly overnight, and forget to lay the groundwork. Undone homework is a dead giveaway, as is a test on the timetable. Novices also fail to prepare the gradual onset of illness, giving a performance worthy of the Royal Shakespeare Company while writhing around in bed and clutching various bits of their anatomy.

Tricks of the trade

Vomit: The only way to be sure that those carrot chunks aren't from a tin of Scotch Broth is to make sure you're always present to witness the upchucking.

Of course, some kids are really dedicated, and rumours always do the rounds at school for the best ways to make yourself throw up for real. Two fingers down the throat is a popular one, as is drinking lots of warm water really quickly. Vinegar and milk is apparently another delightful concoction.

Fever: Many novices will show their hand straight away by complaining that they've got a fever and that they're ever so hot. The educated sickie-taker knows that a fever makes you feel cold. But, there's still the question of faking the internal heat. Again, the mum solution to springing the faker is to be ever vigilant as most of these tricks require a certain amount of privacy, at least for five minutes.

To fake a fever, the thermometer gets dunked in hot cups of tea, held under hot running water, held next to the lightbulb – any nearby heatsource does the trick. Alternatively, drink something as hot as you can bear it and keep the thermometer in the newly warmed mouth as long as possible. Practice makes perfect, though. Too little time at the heat and the mercury will drop right back down again, too long and before you know it ambulances have been called.

Lethargy: OK, so it's hard to know the difference in teenagers, but extra listlessness is supposed to be a sign of illness. Advice doing the rounds suggests kids react with little or no interest to anything that's going on around them. Offers of Playstation or MTV should go barely acknowledged (no gaming? He *must* be sick). Of course, this can backfire into a day of boredom if you're likely to have to stay home with the 'patient' because they won't be able to dash into the living room the moment you've left for work and indulge in their guilty little pleasures. If you suspect a sickie through this method, and the patient already knows that you're going to be home, check in hidey holes for illicit entertainment. This is also true of food.

Loss of appetite: As with lethargy, being off your food is almost a sure sign of some lurgy. If it's genuine then a day of fasting is no big deal. You don't want food so not getting any doesn't matter. But if you're actually well, it's a whole different ball game. Not only are you about to spend the day bored out of your mind, you're going to be starved to death too. And there's nothing like boredom to focus the mind on food. The prepared sickie-taker will therefore have secreted a stash of snacks and drinks somewhere to keep body and soul together.

You don't need to go to huge lengths to uncover a sickie. The promise of some draconian cures should make it clear to the malingering child that, given the choice, going to school is infinitely preferable. If they're genuinely sick, then they'll feel too rotten to care what you do to them.

Chapter Thirteen

Some helpful stuff

arenting gurus are always banging on about how selfless the state of motherhood is, how much us mums sacrifice to raise happy, well-adjusted kids. Well, they're right in terms of sacrifice – these glutes will never see a pair of hotpants again. But that's where it ends.

Heard the saying, 'Why keep a dog and bark yourself?'? Well, it applies to kids, too. There's all this boundless energy, enthusiasm and avarice wrapped up in a 4ft 10in bundle of boredom and you're not going to make use of it? More fool you …

Of course, child slavery is a dreadful thing and not at all what one should be hoping for in modern times. But your average ten year-old will be the first to admit he's not anti the odd car wash if there's a nice crisp fiver in it.

And such is the way of the world. Kids have to do chores, mums have to sit on the sofa watching Audrey Hepburn movies. It all comes down to how much you're willing to pay for the pleasure.

Choreless chores

Pocket money's all very well and good but it's basically money for nothing and that's no good. No good at all. What you need is some cheap labour. By cheap, I mean free.

Well-meaning parenting experts swear by any number of wall charts, happy face stickers, naughty steps and threats of pocket money suspension to get kids to take responsibility for their own filth. Personally, I believe you can't do better than injecting a small dose of fun into chores, coupled with a hefty dollop of bribery.

All of the following chores can be done by one kid on their own and are amazingly involving. However, some do have a competitive element (it encourages them to keep at it longer!) so siblings are handy. If there's only one available child, invite one or more of their mates along. They'll all enjoy it, and you'll get some serious brownie points with their parents, encouraging returned favours down the line.

Slug slaughter

Bought time: at least 30 mins, but with a big garden they could be gone for hours.

To rid the garden of destructive slugs, many gardeners use pellets and sprays. I'm not keen because I don't know what they can do to children and animals. More holistic gardeners swear by beer or salt, claiming that beer sends them off to the happy hunting ground, well, happy. Salt's just plain sadism.

The only really humane way to get rid of the critters is to smash, smush and splat 'em. And kids love it.

Provide old rolling pins (trust me, you don't want to cook with it afterwards) or similar hefty weapons, a box to collect the corpses and a handy pile of change. Offer 10p per slug or snail summarily dispatched. Insist that the bounty hunters only return when they've got at least a quid's worth of bodies, or truly can't find any more.

The promise of filthy lucre should keep them searching for a good while. It isn't cheating if they stray into the neighbour's garden to find more bounty, it's not 10p wasted, it's 10 minutes bought. Settle down with a good book and try to shut out the outdoor massacre with a decent CD.

If you really can't bear the thought of all that smushing, get them to collect live snails instead. Put them in a box with breathing holes in the top. Well, there's no point saving them if you're going to suffocate them to death. Fill it with damp leaves and treat them as pets for a little while.

Prolong the entertainment by setting up some snail races. They can 'go to the farm' after a couple of days. Or, you can all traipse down to the local park and liberate them. Either way, the slimy sods won't be bothering your pansies for a while.

I'm sorry, this does not apply to slugs. It's smushing or nothing for them.

Raking leaves

Bought time: at least 30 minutes.

This chore only applies in autumn and winter, but you could modify it a bit to include grass cuttings or hedge trimmings. You could either pay per bin-bag of leaves, or run a competition between siblings (this can get nasty as one 'sabotages' the other's stash of leaves). Of course, you need to make it slightly amusing by allowing leaf diving and leaf showers before the tidy up begins.

The good thing about leaf collecting, is that no sooner have they finished than one good windy day means they have to start the whole process all over again from scratch.

Clutter chaos

Bought time: varies from 10 minutes to an hour.

Have you ever come back from a weekend away to be amazed at how tidy your house is? That's because no-one's been living in it. Unless you have the cleaning stamina of my mother-in-law, spend more than a few hours together under the same roof and it becomes increasingly hard to find the carpet under all the … stuff.

Of course, simply asking kids to tidy up after themselves is a wholly unimaginative way to go about things. It's also wholly ineffective. Here are two 'carrot and stick' methods to get them to do your dirty work.

Stick: before dinnertime, or a suitable point in the day when they can't claim to be too tired or busy to help, call, 'Clearing – now!' The level of clutter will then determine how long they've got to put everything back in its rightful place. A few games, some cups and a pair of shoes should take about five minutes. A week's worth of gym kit, mouldy packed lunch boxes, a year's worth of *Kerrang!* magazines and a recently bucked Buckeroo means you're in for the long haul.

Warn them how long they've got before you shout, 'Now,' then set a timer – the cooker makes a nice loud beep. Anything that hasn't been put away by the time the beeper goes, gets put in 'Mum's box'. To liberate their possessions from the box, they have to pay a fine. If they get wise to the system and only leave their least wanted rubbish (i.e. school books, Grandma's Christmas jumper) till last, the fine system may fall down. You might want to make sure you're holding on to a valuable piece of clutter (i.e. Xbox controller) to use as a bargaining chip.

Carrot: This is one for more infrequent clear-outs. Get them to sort through toys that they've grown out of or are broken. Ditto comic collections that are gathering dust, and clothes torn beyond repair or too dirty to rescue. Odd socks are a good one too – but check that they're odd, not temporarily divorced.

Then, quite simply, pay them for each item. Set out an agreed price list first:

5p per toy soldier, £1 per intact game, 10p per sock for example. This is purely a monetary arrangement, and can be worked into the pocket money sums if need be (which is why you don't really want to be doing this more than once a month or so).

You then have three options: bin, charity shop or car boot sale/eBay (see below) and to fully earn their cash, the kids have to help with this part too. They can't simply dump the unwanted wares at your feet before vanishing off back to the Playstation.

Graffiti heaven

Bought time: at least two hours. This keeps them going for ages, though you may be expected to view the work in progress from time to time.

Handy if you're planning on redecorating. Pick a wall that you're going to paint anyway. Invest in some coloured tester paint pots from the DIY store, though some of the larger supermarkets stock these too. Most pots have in-built brushes or sponges so you don't need any other equipment. Kids' poster paints work too, but sets of paints and brushes tend to be quite small, and don't give the overall satisfying Rolf Harris effect.

Put down some covering to protect the floor in case the kids decide to unleash their inner Jackson Pollock and tell them to let rip. They can either doodle whatever they want, or you can paint rough squares as a starter and they have to create a different work of art in each, or even a cartoon strip. Seeing as the finished article is inevitably going to get painted a boring magnolia, remember to take a photo of the masterpiece before it's obliterated.

Bonus: Particularly if you're changing colour dramatically, the wall was bound to need a quick undercoat anyway. Once the art exhibition is over, divide up the wall again and start a paint race. Whoever makes it to the middle first wins a prize. But insist that no trace remains. They've got to do a good job!

Depending on how easily satisfied your kids are, the prize can be anything from getting out of cleaning the brushes, to an afternoon watching a favourite DVD in peace or going out for ice cream.

Mini moguls

Bought time: at least a couple of hours with follow-on instalments of half an hour, and riches beyond your wildest dreams!

It's been estimated that the average home has nearly £1,500 worth of unused stuff lying around. The traditional answer used to be to pass it off at Christmas and birthdays to unloved relatives (not that I'd ever do anything like that ...), give it to the charity shop or take it to the car boot sale. Now, there's eBay.

Selling unwanted stuff on eBay is easy-peasy. Take a picture of the unwanted item, write a description of it and stick it online. Someone makes

a bid, you post it off to them and money miraculously appears in your bank account. Hooray! (OK, it's a tad more complex than that, but not much. Visit *www.ebay.co.uk* for the full info.)

Some might think the whole picture-taking, description-writing thing is a bit of a faff. This is where the kids come in. First, get them to find all the things they don't want and pile them up. Obviously, rescue any dubious inclusions like school uniform, your favourite shoes and younger siblings. To be honest, the last of these isn't worth the postage and packing.

They have to take a picture of each article, and then write a description of it. How big it is, what it does, what it originally cost and how much they enjoyed having it.

In deciding how much you want for each item, you have to factor in how much it will cost to post. The Post Office provides a list of costs depending on the weight and size of the item. Get the kids to weigh (kitchen scales do the job fine most of the time, you don't have to be too precise) and measure each piece, and then wrap it up, ready for posting.

In true *Blue Peter* style, they might want an adult to help them with the next bit. Using the online instructions, upload everything to eBay's website. Most listings are on for about seven days so they've got the added excitement of going online and checking how their things are doing.

Once the bid has closed, you are legally bound to send the item so it's time to get down the post office. Depending on the age of your kids, they can go themselves, or they may need a chauffeur. Once posted, all you have to do is wait for the money to roll in.

If you're feeling generous, you might want to let them keep the spoils. It's a good incentive to finally rehome the Scalextric that's been gathering dust in the downstairs cupboard for the last two years. You, of course, keep any cash from Auntie Vi's unwanted ceramic figurines you got as a 'thoughtful gift' last Christmas.

Note, eBay's payment method means that you shouldn't be able to do it unless you're over 18 so don't give them the password, no matter how web-savvy they are.

But they get fifty quid a WEEK!

Just because your adversary still sucks their thumb, it's no excuse not to be fully prepared when entering pocket money negotiations. As a parent, discussions – alright, arguments – with the kids will be peppered with unfavourable comparisons: 'But Appassionata got a pony ...'; 'Harry always stays out in town late ...'. Short of turning Magnum, PI, only experience built up through many mistakes tells you if they're telling porkies.

Helpfully, though, manufacturers of kiddie merchandise are so desperate to get their clammy paws on Francesca's fiver, they've spent millions figuring out exactly how much dough kids these days have to spend. I thought I'd share it with you. That's just the kind of person I am.

Pocket money ready reckoner: average weekly income

Year	7–10-year-olds (£)	11–14-year-olds (£)	15–19-year-olds(£)
2005	3.23	7.51	56.00
2006	3.33	7.90	56.50
2007	3.43	8.10	57.10
2008	3.53	8.20	57.50
2009	3.63	8.30	58.10
2010	3.73	8.40	58.70
2011	3.83	8.60	59.30

Source: Mintel

On average, this means that pocket money goes up by around 7% a year. Unless you're really, really good at your job, or an MP, that's going to be a lot more than your annual raise. And you had to get qualifications and everything. Mind you, it's not only Mum that's getting stiffed for cash.

Who pays?	7–10-year-olds (%)	11–14-year-olds (%)	15–19-year-olds (%)
Mum & Dad	71	77	41
Grandparents	38	26	12
Odd jobs	19	23	–
Elsewhere	19	12	–
Don't get any	6	5	5
Part-time job	–	13	40
Full-time job	–	–	18

Source: Youth TGI, BMRB Spring 2006/Mintel

But Muuuuum ...

If that isn't enough to show them, in black and white, their net worth, it's handy to have a few more facts to hand:

- Three-quarters of children earn pocket money doing jobs around the home.
- A third choose to tidy their rooms for money.
- A third would do general cleaning around the house.
- A third prefer to do the washing up.
- Fagin was right, the younger they are, the more pliable – 69% of 7–11 year olds have to work to earn their pocket money, while only half of 12–16 year olds work for a living.
- On top of pocket money, almost all teenagers get an average of £150 extra a year from gifts or one-off handouts.
- A busy 14% of 16+ year olds manage to earn more than £500 a month through odd jobs and other sources. Notably, parental contributions by this point pretty much dry up.

The going rate

Depending on how tight a grip you've managed to keep on the purse strings, you can approach the 'money for labour' idea in two ways.

Either, you set out a list of chores as part of daily life and if they're all completed to your satisfaction, pocket money is duly paid. This is probably the approach favoured by do-gooding child psychologists who never have to bribe kids to get out of bed in the morning.

Alternatively, you can pay per job, on a cash-in-hand basis. On the upside, you have more bargaining power when it comes to getting something done (no job, no money). On the downside, you could be nurturing a 'minipreneur', who is content to work as hard as the day is long to relieve you of every last cent.

Finally, you can offer extra jobs cash in hand on top of normal pocket money to help the kids save for that little something extra.

In any case, here is a list of jobs and age ranges. Try comparing notes with fellow parents to get a consensus on the going rate, and fill in the boxes opposite. Then you have incontrovertible proof that Jimbo from number 33 isn't getting 15 quid a week to keep his bedroom tidy.

These are 2007 prices. Remember your compound interest calculations of 7% pa for the future. Or bung an extra 50p in every other year.

I did some wide-ranging research on the topic (OK, I asked a few friends) and there were some startling answers. One claimed that she was paid to darn her dad's socks at 12p a pop. She also noted that she babysat her brother and sister all day, including trips to the park. For this, she was handsomely paid with three fingers of fudge. She now feels that her parents were somewhat sucked in by the ad strapline of the day, which promised: 'A finger of fudge is just enough to give your kids a treat.' Try paying today's ten-year-olds for six hours work with three 10p sticks of chocolate and see where it gets you …

Another was more richly rewarded for her toils. She was gainfully employed making gin and tonics for her grandmother at 50p a time. She omitted to mention if Granny was a particularly thirsty lady.

Job	7–10	11–14	15–19
Washing the car			
Taking the rubbish out			
Emptying the cat litter			
Walking the dog			
Tidying the bedroom			
Trimming the hedge			
Picking fruit and veg			
Babysitting (legal from age 14)			
Painting a wall			
Clearing snow from the drive			
Fetching the shopping			
Washing up			
Cutting the grass			
Sweeping up leaves			
Dusting			

Appendix One

Essential stuff

There are some skills that our mother's mothers passed onto them, their mothers before them, and their mothers before them and so on. But for some reason, there doesn't seem to have been an awful lot of passing down from the last generation to this one. Ladies, many of us are sorely lacking in mum skills.

There are umpteen skills that our mothers and grandmothers had that we have absolutely no need of today. Even everyday annoyances that haven't changed since the middle ages have a modern solution. Dropped hems can be fixed with wonderwebbing; blackcurrant stains can be got out with magnificent washing powders or, as is often the case, it's just as cheap to replace the item altogether.

But what if you don't want to buy a new shirt, or your hem's come down two hours before the wedding and the shops are shut? Wouldn't it be handy to know the good old-fashioned way of sorting it out? What about inviting friends round for dinner – do you always want to give them something you reheated in the microwave?

And then of course there's women's lib. Sometime around the 1970s, everyone finally realised that there was no specific reason why women should be better at washing up or hoovering than men. In an age of equal opportunities, I fully expect my kids' dad to be able to fix their supper as well as their bikes.

This chapter's all about knowing how to do 'Mum Stuff', just because you can. And best of all, if you want to get someone else to do it, you can show them how before putting your feet up and let them get on with it.

Nursery food

Everyone has a meal that they turn to for comfort. If you want some proper comfort food look no further than nursery food – so-called because it's the sort of easy, bland, but ultimately reassuring food you were given as a child.

It's also the sort of five-minute meal that you make for your kiddies but that no self-respecting student should leave home without knowing. Partly to stave off homesickness, but also partly because every recipe is almost entirely dependent on eggs, bread and cheese – all being cheap, hard to screw up and readily available down the 24-hour garage.

French toast/eggy bread

> 1 egg
> 1 tablespoon sugar
> 1 slice bread
> Knob of butter

Beat the egg and sugar together. Dip the bread in the mix so that it's well coated and the mix soaks in. Transfer to a hot frying pan (if it's good and hot you shouldn't need any oil) and fry until both sides are golden. Drop a small knob of butter on the hot toast and munch. Wait for arteries to close.

Eggs in a basket

> Knob of butter
> 1 slice of bread
> 1 egg

Gently melt the butter in a frying pan. Cut a hole from the inside of the slice of bread (use a glass or a cup if you don't have a cutter) and place in frying pan. Carefully break an egg into the middle. Fry gently (not as hot as for French toast) and serve. Flip and cook both sides if you like your eggs 'over easy'. Personally, I prefer breaking into that lovely yolky blister.

Eggs in a nest

    4 ovenproof ramekins
    butter
    1lb potatoes, mashed
    4 eggs
    milk or cream
    grated cheese

Grease the inside of the ramekins with a little butter, and fill with mashed potato, leaving a 'well' in the middle. Break an egg into the well and splash a little milk (about a tablespoon) on top. Put a small knob of butter on top of the egg, scatter cheese round the edges of the cheese and cook in the oven at 200°C for 10 minutes, or until the egg is cooked.

Eggies in a cup

    3 large eggs
    butter
    salt

Soft boil 3 eggs (my technique is to get the water boiling and put the eggs in gently and time 5 generous minutes. Also I keep eggs in the cupboard not the fridge so they don't crack). Scoop the insides out into a mug and add a generous knob of butter and a pinch of salt. Bash up and eat out of the mug with a teaspoon. Use your finger to scoop up the last of the yolky goodness.

Macaroni cheese/cauliflower cheese

    1 heaped dessertspoon butter
    1 heaped dessertspoon plain flour
    150g grated mature cheddar
    150ml milk
    2 tsp English mustard
    pepper
    macaroni or cauliflower

Melt the butter in a pan. Sprinkle flour over the top and mix together with a wooden spoon. It should make a round, buttery lump of dough in the bottom of the pan. If it doesn't, chuck in another spoonful of flour.

When the butter and flour are mixed, add in the milk bit by bit, stirring all the time. When the mixture is the consistency of anaemic custard, add in grated cheese and stir until melted. Taste and if it's not cheesey enough, grate in more cheese. Bring gently to the boil until the texture thickens a bit more and becomes quite … sauce-like. Add in mustard and season with pepper to taste.

Boil a handful of dried macaroni or cauliflower per person, then put in an ovenproof dish. Cover with cheese sauce and grated cheese and bung under the grill until the top is crispy. Eat watching *Doctor Who* from behind the sofa.

Banana sandwiches

> 1 ripe banana
> 2 slices brown bread
> sunflower spread

For some reason, this just doesn't work with white bread or butter. You need the maltiness of the brown bread and the saltiness of the spread to make it just right. Simply slice or mash the banana with a fork and make a sandwich. Cut into halves and devour.

Trifle

> 1 pack sponge fingers
> 1 tin fruit salad
> 1 pack raspberry jelly
> 1 pack instant custard
> Squirty cream
> Chopped nuts or hundreds and thousands
> Sherry for the over 18s only

You could faff about with homemade elderberry jelly and crème anglaise and freshly picked raspberries and homemade Madeira cake but life's too short and the slightly plastic taste of all the processed ingredients is somehow more ... authentic.

Get a big bowl and lay out a layer of sponge fingers. Pour over half the juice from the fruit salad and put another layer of sponge on top. Pour the rest of the juice over. Then tip the fruit out and spread out evenly. Make up the jelly as per the packet instructions and allow to cool before pouring on top of the fruit (you want it to be on the verge of setting so that it doesn't soak too much into the sponge). Put in the fridge to set.

Make up the custard as per instructions, leave to cool a little then pour onto the set jelly. Put back in fridge. Once this has set, cover in a generous layer of squirty cream and scatter with nuts or hundreds and thousands.

If you're making the grown-up version, pour a medium sherry such as Bristol Cream all over the sponge until it looks like it can take no more. Then pile everything else on top as described. Serve firsts, then seconds.

'Full beans, half cheese'

1 small tin baked beans

1 large handful grated cheddar

This is how I used to order my lunch at school in Edinburgh. It literally meant a ladleful of baked beans and half a serving of grated cheese. Absolutely the simplest thing to make but it would leave me warmed and happy for hours. I still make it if I'm feeling chilly or poorly on the sofa. Microwave the beans in a mug until they're nice and hot. Add the grated cheese on the top. Smush about with a teaspoon until the cheese is all melted in and eat in front of the telly.

Bacon and cheese

vegetable oil

4 slices bacon cut into strips

1 medium onion, chopped

boiling water

113g (4oz) of strong cheddar cheese

2–4 slices of thick firm bread

This is a recipe from the Second World War, designed to make use of leftovers such as cheese rinds and bits of bacon or a gammon joint. Heat a frying pan and add a small amount of oil to gently fry the bacon. After a few minutes add the chopped onion and continue to fry gently, making sure you don't burn the onions. Cover this with about a half-inch of boiling water and let it simmer. The grated cheese can be added until it melts. Stir continuously to distribute the cheese around the bacon and onions, pour onto thick bread and scoff, loudly.

Real Food

Mum's ultimate meal

Mum in her pinny and a steaming joint of meat may be a 1950s cliché, but it's also a really powerful reminder of hearth and home and it's exactly the sort of thing your kids will pine for when they're stuck in student digs with a tin of beans and no opener.

The traditional Sunday roast seems to strike fear into the most confident cook. I can't see why. Trust me, it's easy. Even the scary Yorkshire pudding bit. Take it from someone who has burnt and then blown up three boiled eggs.

Roast beef with all the trimmings (serves 4)

the meat
5lb (2.5kg) beef on the bone (sirloin or rib)
large roasting tin

the Yorkshire
3oz/75g plain flour
1 egg

3fl oz/75ml milk
2fl oz/50ml water
oil or lard
pie dish/muffin tray

the sides

desiree or King Edward potatoes
green beans
broccoli

the gravy

red wine
beef or vegetable stock
3 garlic cloves
Dijon or English mustard
redcurrant jelly

the maths

put the meat in the oven at:

20 mins	gas mark	9/245°C
then		
15 mins	per lb/450g	Rare
plus		
15 mins extra		Medium rare
or		
30 mins extra		Well-done
finally		
30 mins to relax*		

*the beef, not the chef, unfortunately. Take it out of the oven and lay it somewhere out of the reach of family pets and Dad.

A rare treat at 2 p.m. sharp

Here's how it works if you want the roastie and its trimmings all ready at the same time. Before you do anything, put the oven on. It needs time to heat up before you start.

12 noon Put seasoned beef in the oven on the middle shelf. You want to leave enough space on the top shelf of your oven to slide the roast potatoes in. Set timer for 20 minutes at gas mark 9/245°C.

Peel and chop potatoes. Cut up half the quantity into eighths for mash, and the other half into quarters for roasting. Put two pans of salted water on to boil.

12.20 p.m. Turn the oven down to gas mark 5/190°C. Set timer for 65 minutes. Put both sets of potatoes into each pan of boiling water for 10 minutes.

12.30 p.m. Drain potatoes and leave to one side. Make Yorkshire pudding batter:

Put the flour in a bowl and make a well in the middle. Break the egg into the well and start to beat the flour into the egg. Gradually add the milk and water along with salt and pepper. Leave aside. It will be ready to go in the oven at 1.25 p.m.

You have half an hour to kill – wine break!

You may also want to take the time to clear up some of the cooking mess made up to now. Dealing with the final stages is easier if you have clear space to use. This is particularly true of pans that mount up with frightening speed.

Of course, this is an ideal moment to rope in a few willing volunteers …

1 p.m. In a flameproof dish on the hob, heat a couple of tablespoons of oil until sizzling.

Quickly put the potatoes for roasting into the oil and turn with a fork or tongs (or fingers for the brave) until coated.

Put roast potatoes into the oven for 60 minutes or until crispy and golden. Turn from time to time to make sure they cook evenly on all sides.

1.25 p.m. Take beef out and move to a plate, leaving the juices in the roasting dish. Turn the oven up to 220°C/gas mark 7.

Heat oil in a muffin tin or pie dish until sizzling hot. If your joint was quite oily you might want to use a couple of tablespoons from that because it'll give a nice taste to the Yorkie. Pour in the Yorkshire batter and put on the shelf below the potatoes. Set the timer for 30 minutes.

1.30 p.m. Pour milk and butter into the potatoes for mashing, turn on a gentle heat and pound. When mashed, turn off heat, replace lid, leave to stand.

1.40 p.m. Put fresh vegetables such as cauliflower or broccoli into boiling salted water and simmer for 20 minutes.

1.50 p.m. If using frozen vegetables such as cauliflower, broccoli or green beans, simmer for between 8–15 minutes depending on packaging instructions.

Pour any new juices that have just run out of the resting beef into the roasting tin. Place the tin over a medium heat on the hob and when it begins to bubble add your gravy ingredients. Stir and season to taste.

1.55 p.m. Take Yorkshire pudding and roast potatoes out of oven and place on the table on a heatproof mat.

Drain vegetables and give a quick blast of ice-cold water. Toss into big bowls with a generous lump of butter, a sprinkling of salt and pepper and send them through to join the Yorkshire and roast potatoes.

Spoon mash into a bowl, again with the butter, salt and pepper and off to the table it goes.

2.00 p.m. Process to the table with the beef in a great flourish, hand the job of carving to someone else (preferably of at least senior school age) and sit down, glass in hand, ready to receive praise and adoration from all.

Top tips

- For perfect roast spuds, put the lid on the pan and shake for a few seconds. This breaks up the outside of the potatoes and helps your roasts have a nice crispy, light skin.

- Never be tempted to use a hand blender or electronic whisk to take lumps out of potatoes. They turn to glue and it's not a pleasant texture to eat. A quick fix if this happens – keep Smash in the larder!

- Have a bowl of cold water with a couple of ice cubes in it ready to plunge the sieve with the vegetables into. This stops them cooking and going that horrible, soggy grey-green but keeps them hot enough to eat.

- Putting hot food into cold bowls soon makes the food cold too. Use serving bowls and plates as pan lids so that the steam from the cooking vegetables warms them at the last minute. For the gravy jug, warm with boiling water from the kettle a few moments before you plan to pour in the gravy.

So sewing

The majority of everyday clothes these days are so affordable and easily replaceable, there is little need to darn, mend, take in or up any more. Thank God.

But not everything can be bought or replaced at the drop of a hat. What about torn hems, too-big skirts and fancy dress outfits? If you're a complete stranger to a needle and thread, you commit yourself to a lifetime of alteration bills and the sequin-splattered hell of the Disney store.

Stitch styles

To get cloth to hold together, you really only need two stitches – tacking and backstitch. Everything else is embroidery.

Tacking

This is used when you want to keep two bits of cloth together more reliably than using pins but you want it to be easy and quick to remove when you're finished. It's typically used when making clothes so that they're easy to try on and alter before the proper stitches are sewn.

Simply, sew along the seam using biggish stitches. They don't need to be neat and you don't need to fix them securely so just a knot at one end will do the trick.

Backstitch

Take one stitch and then repeat it in the same place, so you have two stitches going through the same place. For real security, you can sew a third stitch but be careful not to make the cloth bunch up. Unless it's something that's going to take a lot of strain like a button or a fat tummy, you shouldn't need more than two.

Hemstitch

Turn the piece of clothing inside out so you can see the open hem. Pin it to hold it in place. At the very edge of the hem put the needle through from front to back. Then, before pulling it all the way through, use the very tip of the needle and try to pick up a tiny thread from the fabric of the clothes. Then pull the thread through. Keep going all the way round the hem.

You can make the stitch as bold as you like going through the edge of the hem, but you want to make sure you're picking up the smallest bit of thread on the main bit of the garment. Then, when you turn it right side out, you shouldn't be able to see anything, perhaps the slightest pin head of thread and maybe a slight puckering (dimpling) that will be sorted out by the iron.

There are a whole bunch of magic products out there that you simply iron in and hey presto, a pristine hem. They're great for an area that gets no strain and isn't going to be washed very much but that's their limit. When it comes to trouser legs, they just don't hold up.

Sewing on a button

When (not if) a button comes off, two things are guaranteed. One: it will instantly be lost forever. Don't waste time looking for it. Two: it will be front and centre on your shirt or coat so your intrinsic buttonlessness will be there for all to see. To remedy this, take a button from the least conspicuous part of the garment and transplant it to where the missing one should be. You can then use a closeish match for the unobtrusive area and no-one should really notice. Other than your mother-in-law.

The technique:

Do up the remaining buttons to make sure you're going to put the missing button in the right place. Centre it and make sure the holes in the button match up with the buttons above and below it. Nothing screams mending than skew-whiff holes.

Depending on the style of button, it may have two or four holes, or a hoop at the back. In each case, using strong thread and beginning from the wrong side of the fabric go in and out of the holes about six times each. Finish on the wrong side of the fabric and do a couple of backstitches to make sure it doesn't unravel.

Tip: Putting a pin, matchstick or toothpick between the button and the fabric ensures that you don't sew it on so tight that you can't manipulate the button to do it up.

Fixing a zip

It can be done, but in my opinion life's just too short. Mending broken zips is fiddly, difficult and rarely successful when done by the layman. Often it involves removing the broken zip completely and replacing it with a new one. Today's mass production machining means that tampering with one seam on a garment can quite often lead to the disastrous unravelling of the whole thing. When the zip goes on a beloved, utterly irreplaceable or expensive item, then by all means take it to the menders. It'll be worth the investment.

Stain removal

Stain alive

Having spent much of Chapter Two showing you how to get a variety of fruit, vegetable and animal colours into cloth and skin, now you need to know how to get them out. The first thing to say is that modern detergents do a pretty good job, and given the right circumstances there isn't much they can't get out of a school shirt.

However, a lot also depends on the item going straight from staining incident to washing drum and that's not always possible. When camping in the Malvern hills, not everyone has access to their Washerator 5000 with extra spin and muck-removal function. And, somehow, cubes of Pixie-

Smurf-Parcel super-suds just don't seem to work as well in a bucket of cold water from the campsite loos.

Not all of these muck-removing solutions need be used on the hoof, but they're good to know.

Bubble gum/chewing gum

One of the biggest problems is the 'bubble gum in hair' look. Trying to get this stuff out with a brush elicits screams unheard of since you tried to put you five-year-old bed-head in neat plaits for Grandma's visit. **Top tip:** pour motor oil over the offending area and gently brush it out. OK, so you can use more pleasant smelling oils like coconut or almond. Even peanut butter seems to do the trick. But motor oil seems like such a good punishment for getting gum stuck there in the first place.

Other common gum disasters include getting it stuck to furniture carpets and clothes. In this case, try using ice that should freeze the gum hard, making it easier to break off. Don't use oil on this occasion because getting oil out of fabric and wood is a total pain …

Oil stains

Some advise putting the affected material on brown paper and sandwiching it between towels before ironing the stain out. This may work, but equally it may 'fix' the stain in place by cooking it. If it's only a little spill, dab on some liquid detergent before washing it in the machine on the hottest cycle the fabric will stand. Big spills should be put on paper towels, with a good stain-remover cleaning fluid squirted all over the back of the stain. Change the paper towels over until they appear to have soaked up the majority of the stain. Hang out to dry completely, rinse again then wash in the hottest cycle it can stand.

Grass stains

Use a stain-removing product to pretreat it. If the stain's still there, try sponging it with alcohol (the rubbing, not the red wine kind). Then, as a last ditch attempt, wash on the hottest cycle possible with a bleaching agent if you don't think it will affect the colour of the fabric.

Coffee/tea

Dip it immediately into cold water. Soak for a further 30 minutes in cool water, rub with liquid detergent and wash as usual.

Ketchup

Rinse in cold water and soak in a cool, weak detergent solution (10ml per litre of water). Pretreat if possible with a stain remover and wash as usual.

Crayons/candlewax

This is the stain to get the iron onto, but not straight away. Harden any excess wax with ice and scrape as much away as possible. Sandwich between paper towels and press gently with a warm iron. Keep changing all the paper towels until the candlewax or crayon wax is out of the cloth. Sponge with a stain remover, blot with more kitchen towel and let it dry before washing on a hot cycle.

Blood

Soak the fresh stain in cold water for 30 minutes. Rub washing powder (or liquid) into whatever is left and then wash. For dried stains, soak in a dedicated stain remover then wash, but in both cases, only use cold water as hot will 'cook' the stain into the cloth for good. However, once you've done the pre-treating it's okay to wash in warm water.

Ink

You can try soaking in cold water and gently rubbing with a bit of detergent, but there are also special treatments on the market depending on the kind of pen. Beware that many inks may be in there for good. Now is the time to tell you that there are many art materials on the market that have "washable" on the front in big letters. There's a reason they sell so well!

Keeping stuff

The whole point of making things using the stuff lying around the house is that: it's already lying around the house. You shouldn't have to go out and buy any special equipment for most of the ideas in the book.

That said ... Some things will be a lot easier to make if you invest in a few handy items. There's nothing more frustrating than the sudden urge to make Thunderbirds' Tracey Island when they're making it right there on the telly, and hearing cries of, 'Why-don't-we-have-any-PVA-glue-and-no-Pritt Stick? It isn't-good-enough-*Muuuum*!'

There are three categories of stuff:

Hoard

Things you need to squirrel away as and when you come across them because they'll come in useful later.

- Old tights, knee-highs are good too
- Old tennis balls, even if they've been pre-mauled by Fido
- Toilet and kitchen roll innards
- Bits of string
- Old clothes, especially colourful cottons and jumpers
- Washing-up bottles
- Glass jars, with or without lids
- Blank forms from the bank and post office
- Coloured tissue from clothes shops
- Old stamps

- Foreign money
- Elastic bands
- Takeaway tins or tubs (plastic and metal are best)
- Cereal boxes
- Cheese triangle round boxes
- String and rope
- Fizzy pop bottles
- Remnants of wool
- Used computer printouts (preferably still blank on one side)
- Newspapers (with the amount of supplements these days, a couple of Sundays-worth should do the trick)

Borrow

Someone you know will own a mallet/saw/sugar thermometer.
Kid's projects are not an excuse for extravagant, niche retail therapy.

- Electric drills
- Mallets
- Sugar Thermometers
- Big Pans
- Other people's houses

Buy

Cheap odds and ends that make the whole 'homemade' extravaganza much less painful.

- PVA glue
- Glitter
- Poster/acrylic paints
- Cheapo felt pens
- A pen for marking freezer bags
- Pritt stick

- Coloured tissue paper/coloured paper napkins
- Decent scissors
- Sewing needles – a mixed pack
- Knitting needles
- White thread
- Black thread
- A cheap milk pan
- Black bin bags
- Plasticine
- Sellotape and double-sided sticky tape

Appendix Three

Remembering stuff

Some of the ideas in this book have come from mums, others from grans, granddads, aunties … even dads. Others come via our friends on the Internet and strangers in the supermarket queue. Either way, most have been handed down from one generation to the next in that great verbal tradition.

Unfortunately, this method means that far more gets forgotten than is remembered by both the hander-down and the handee. Here's your opportunity to capture that wisdom for ever. Grill your own mum, or uncle or whoever has a great idea and use these scant pages to set them in stone (or recycled tree as most paper is these days) for generations to come.

It might be a key to your own family version of Pig Latin (see page 110), or a magic gravy recipe that's just the dog's danglies (see page 222). Perhaps your family has five more innovative uses for a pair of 40 deniers that weren't covered in the 12 things to do with a pair of tights section.

Fair enough, mum wisdom is more usually of the 'If you break your leg, don't come running to me' variety, but sometimes, just sometimes, there's a little bit of gold dust …

Index

Acknowledgements

With thanks to:

Angela Herlihy for going with it in the first place, then along with Martin Lovelock and Liane Payne for making it look beautiful – and make sense! And to the wonderful Sue Hellard, whose gorgeous illustrations make Mum come alive. Her Mum is a little bit scatty, a little bit scruffy, a little bit out of control and a little bit gorgeous. She's a little bit of all of us.

I also want to thank the small army that proved inspiration for the book:

Rebecca S, Patrick and Sam for tea, choo-choos and more wine than is good for anyone.

Marianne, Tim and Freya for biscuits, Teletubbies and yet more wine.

Paula and Gabriel for all the mad emails and yes, even more wine.

Ruth, Maeve, Rebecca D and Kate for ideas, inspiration and putting up with my incessant whingeing and need for donuts (sugar substitute. Apparently, you can't drink wine in the office).

Phil, Aaron, James but especially Lisa for keeping Tom under control and dispensing words of encouragement when the will to hit the library was waning.

Sian and Arnold for the gushings of praise when there wasn't even a single word on paper.

Dad for always telling me that if you don't ask, you don't get.

Harriet and Emily for the ever eloquent exclamation: "S 'mazin'!'

Gran for her encouragement and off-the-wall ideas.

Mum for the ability to knit, read, watch the telly and hold a conversation all at the same time. She invented multi-tasking!

Special thanks to Tomos for giving me the idea, the early-morning alarm calls and his own special way of dancing to Madonna that cracks us all up.

But above all, thanks and awe are due to my husband, Dylan, who became chief cook, cleaner, kid-wrangler, driver, psychiatrist and all-round super stud while I locked myself in my garrett. I couldn't have done it without you and you are a legend. Does this mean I have to start doing the washing-up again now?

Love and homemade bramble jam to you all,

Morag